Computer Survival Kit for Seniors and Beginners Revision 2

by

Dr. Alfonso J. Kinglow PhD

Copyright © 2021 Alfonso J. Kinglow

All rights reserved.

ISBN: 978-1-257-98424-4

Library of Congress Control Number: 2020901664

Printed in The United States of America

DEDICATION

I would like to dedicate this book to all the Seniors of Shadow Mountain Senior Center in Phoenix Arizona, and to my wife of 44 years for her Support and Love and all my Grand Children for making me a Grandfather and a better man, during this Pandemic.

CONTENTS

	Acknowledgments	i
1	Basic Hardware and Software	Pg # 1
2	Computer Security Setup	Pg # 123
3	What is a Computer	Pg # 9
4	The ALU Configurations with Windows 10 Graphics	Pg # 146 Pg #148
5	Computer System Cleaning Tools	Pg # 26
6	Basic Computer Glossary	Pg # 29
7	Basic User Tools What is a Virus	Pg # 152 Pg #154
8	More Performance from Windows and Appearance	Pg # 154 - 167
9	Shutdown Windows Correctly	Pg # 163
10	Hidden Codes in Windows	Pg # 162

11	Extended Hidden Codes	Pg # 180
12	Shutdown Windows Tool	Pg #177-178
13	The CMD and MMC	
14	Command and Diagnostics	Pg#163-166
15	Windows Shortcuts and Utilities and User Tools.	Pg#168-169
16	Extended System Tools and Admin Tools	Pg#171-172
17	Explorer Shell and Services	Pg#173-174

ACKNOWLEDGMENTS

I would like to Thank all the Staff and Supervisors of **Shadow Mountain Senior Center, in Phoenix Arizona** for all the Help in providing a Room and Facilities to Teach the Computer Classes over the years, and for caring, and the excellent work they do for the Seniors of Phoenix every day. Thank you Tyler, and all the Staff for the caring and the great Job you do to support us the Seniors and Volunteers, specially during this time of Pandemic.
Thank You

1 BASIC HARDWARE AND SOFTWARE

One of the main problems that Seniors and Beginners Computers may have, is that they are not configured correctly and may have the absolute minimum hardware for the Operating Systems they are using, like all the different versions of Windows 10 and or other OS., They may have a Windows version that is not the correct one for them.

So, what is **The Basic Configuration** that Seniors and Beginners should have, to avoid problems and be ready for the unexpected.

Let us consider the **Hardware first.** Most new Computers will have the absolute minimum hardware configuration, and maybe the right Operating System, like Windows OS but it does not mean that they will work OK for the User(s).

The Software or Operating System on the new Computer may be the absolute minimum wrong OS for the Computer, does not matter which Brand of Hardware.
The Computer Stores just want to sell the Computer and they do not care if its the wrong configuration for the user needs.

So as Users, we must have the Knowledge and be intelligent enough to ask for the correct system that we want and need, to do the job we want, at Home or at Work.

BASIC COMPUTER SPECIFICATION

The correct minimum Hardware System you should have:

The CPU: The CPU or Central Processing Unit should be above 2.0 GHz or 2.7 GHz, 2.8 GHz, 3.0 GHz or higher. This will determine the SPEED of your Computer.

The higher the GHz (Gigahertz) the faster the Computer. The Computer will be very SLOW if the CPU is below 2.0 GHz, like 1.5 GHz, 1.7 GHz or 1.8 GHz etc..
This should be the first thing to look out for.
Don't buy Computers with Low CPU Speed. Below 2.0 GHz.

The Computer RAM Memory should be: 8 GB (Gigabytes); or 16 GB or higher. The absolute minimum should be 8 GB.
Don't buy Computers with 2 GB, **3 GB**, 4 GB, **6GB** of RAM Memory. Some Computers come with ODD Memory, like **3 GB** or **6GB**; that are wrong, and does not conform to the International Standards of Memory Configuration; 2,4,8,16,32,64,128 GB etc..

The Speed of your Computer is determined by the CPU and the RAM Memory in its correct configuration.

The Hard Drive or **C:>** Drive (HD) is where all of your Software and Operating System (OS) Windows versions are installed., with your own personal files and Applications, and will require large amount of Space or Storage.

The absolute minimum HD Space should be **1** to

1.5 T bytes or (tb) terabytes or more.
Do not buy computers with GB (gigabyte) Hard Drives, such as 500 GB or 800 GB. You will run out of Space in no time. Most Application Programs today are 300 GB or more, just to install them on the Hard Drive(s).

The Hard Drive is also called, " The Storage Area".. Where all of the User files are Stored..
 The main hard drive on the Computer is called the **C:>** drive, and must be kept Clean from Viruses and Junk that will Slow down its performance and access.

 Free utilities are available to the Users that will **Defragment** the Hard drive. Files Stored on the Hard Drive will tend to **Fragment over time,** and will slow down the access of important files and applications.

Cleaning the Hard drive once a week will preserve the access speed and protect the files.

The Cleaning Utility for the HD is called: **SMART DEFRAG version 6.7** and can be downloaded from the Internet **Free.**
Install Smart Defrag 6.7 on the computer and run it once a week, to keep the Hard Drive Files from Fragmenting.

On most Hard Drives, Fragmentation will happen when files and applications are stored on the drive, and the information is broken up in parts to save space, so the file may be Stored in groups called **Bits and Bytes.**
Eight Bits (8 bits= 1 Byte.)

Bits are Stored all over the drive.. **One BIT** is the smallest unit of information that can be Stored or Transmitted. Its a **Binary number** representing **Zero (0) or One (1).**

The Ethernet Network Card or (NIC), and WI-Fi Card are very important and critical on the Computer. A poor Network Card will produce a Slow-Internet and Network connection. It is recommended that the Ethernet Card be Gigabit Ethernet speed., for Standard Internet operation.

The minimum Ethernet Network Card should support 100 Mbps or (100 Megabits per sec.) the basic Internet Standard Speed.

The Internet WI-Fi Card minimum should be:
The card should be an 802.11 a/b/g/**n** as a bare minimum, it is recommended that **the Network Card be for higher Speed of 802.11a/b/g/ac**   for Gigabit and/or 802.11 a/b/g/**ad or ax** for much higher Internet Speeds.

Most Network Cards are going to be of the type (**n**) in most computers that are sold today, with a Frequency of only **2.4 GHz.,** which is slow, however; Users can UPGRADE to a fast Network of frequency 2.4GHz plus (+) a **5 GHz Dual Band** 802.11 **AC** High Speed with MU-MIMO support by using the ASUS USB-Wi-Fi ADAPTER AC1200 USB-AC53 Nano; for less than US.$20.00, from Amazon.
This little **USB Plug-In** will triple your Internet Speed, without having to change or buy a new NIC Network Adapter Card. This will give the Users access to the **5GHz** Band for Networking at high Speed.

Your Internet Router for example, will then show the number (2) beside your **Router Name;** like:Netgear N2345 -2 indicating the access of the new **5GHz** Internet Band.

Your Wi-Fi **available Networks** will show two Netgear N2345 Routers, with the second one having the **(2)** beside it which will be your **5 GHz Band. Select the 5 GHz Band for high speed.**

Do not get Computers with slow Internet Cards that are only 802.11 a/b/g/**n if you do;** you can always buy the ASUS Adapter to access the **5GHz** high speed **802.11 AC.**

The International Standard for Networks is 802.11 for Wireless and 802. 3 for Wired Ethernet.

In most Computers the NIC or Network Cards are also called; **Network Adapters.** Most Computers will have two (2) Network Cards, one Ethernet Card and another a WI-Fi Card for Wireless Internet connection.

The Computer Graphics Card, should support the basic Video configuration of **1024 X 768 Resolution** or higher.
The minimum Video Screen Display should be 15 inches or higher to 17 inches for Laptops and much larger for Monitors, all the way to 50 -75 inches.

The basic Memory for Graphics Card, such as the ENVIDIA Brand, can be 64 GB to 128 GB or higher.
To support HI-RES Displays.

2 WINDOWS 10 VERSIONS

They are several versions of Windows 10 Operating System also called, the Windows OS. If you buy a Computer today, most basic computers will come with **WINDOWS HOME or WINDOWS BASIC.**

These versions will be <u>the absolute minimum versions</u> of Windows OS, they will not have some features that most basic Users need. And installed on a new Computer hardware, will be useless., and **Not recommended.**

The Windows 10 version Users should have and /or buy depending on the type of Computers are:

WINDOWS 10 STANDARD EDITION
WINDOWS 10 BASIC EDITION
WINDOWS 10 PROFESSIONAL = Recommended

Other Versions of Windows 10:

Windows 10 Home Edition = Not Recommended
Windows 10 Student Edition
Windows 10 Business Edition
Windows 10 Education Edition
Windows 10 Enterprise Edition
Windows 10 Client Server Edition
Windows 10 Core Edition

3 WHAT IS A COMPUTER

Basic information every User should know.

A Computer consist of Hardware and Software. The Hardware contains the Memory, Storage and CPU, the Mouse and Keyboard and the Video Display with many internal parts like the Network Adapter and the Video Graphics Card and DVD player.

The Software is the program that runs the Computer Hardware, it is called the System Software or the Operating System. In this case the Operating System is a **GUI** (Graphic User Interface) type called **Windows.**

The other many Software that runs on the Computer are called: Applications, Utilities, Programs, Diagnostics, Administrative, System, User Programs, and Tools.

Computers are Digital Machines and use their own Computer Language called Binary Language, that represents (0) zero and (1) one.
Computers began in the Analog World and we can say Computers are divided into Digital and Analog.

Analog Computers needed a Cable to communicate between computers, by sending a Signal (Sound Wave) or **Sine Wave.** If the Cable was too long, then the Signal would Degrade. Coaxial Cable was used to preserve the Signal, and two Cables were used. The Transmit Cable and the Receive Cable. Zero (0) Decibels or Zero db. At 600 Ohms Termination, was used as a Standard for Testing and

Transmitting and Receiving a signal. The zero Decibel Signal was generated by an Electronic Device called an Oscillator produced by a Vacuum Tube called a TRIODE that consisted of a Plate, Grid and Filaments.

Somewhere after 1965 aprox. The Digital Signal was discovered and Developed by IBM, SPARK, Xerox, DEC and others., and the Digital Era began.

An IC or Integrated Circuit Chip was built called an A/D and a D/A Chip. Analog to Digital and Digital to Analog Converters. An Analog Signal could then be converted to Digital Form using 0 zero and one (1) and a **Square Wave** was born.

The **Square Wave** is a Binary Signal that starts from **zero** then rises to **1 volt,** with a time of **1 sec** then dropping to **zero** again., a Binary number is then created, or 010. This Binary number is called a **BIT,** and represents zero (0) or one (1), OFF/ON. Therefore; the smallest Unit of Information that can be Transmitted is a **BIT.**

Computers using zero's and one's to communicate, or bits per second (bps) form a BINARY LANGUAGE, used by Computers all over the World.

Because the **BIT** is very small, it was organized into more larger and manageable sizes that would handle the large and vast requirements for **Storage and Memory,** so STANDARDS had to be created.
The Standard for **MEMORY** begins with 1 Gb, then 2-4-8-16-32-64-128-256-512-**1024 Gb**. (Giga-Bytes)etc..

Computers with 3 and 6 Gigabytes are not recommended; as Memory works in Equal Pairs. Eight Gigabytes (8 Gb.) should be **4Gb + 4Gb = 8 Gb.**
 The Beginning.__   IBM – XEROX – SPARK – DEC.

IBM first PC, The IBM Pcjr also called The Rainbow Computer, was the result of the Digital Era.

THE ANALOG WORLD. ____

A) The ANALOG Wave is a SINE WAVE or Audio Signal that is SINO SUOIDAL or Low sound to high sound back to low sound.. Going from 0 (zero) signal to One (1) High Signal., measured in CYCLES PER SECOND., (CPS); also called HERTZ, Hz. Named after Heinrich Hertz (German Physicist) who discovered it.

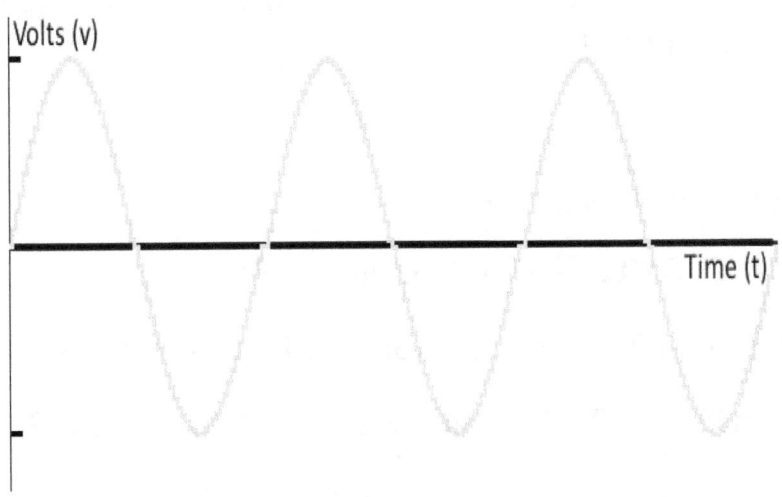

The SPEED of the Signal is Measured in Hz. Or Cycles - per-Second (cps). The Computer (CPU) Central Processing Unit, is measured in Giga-hertz or GHz.

Example:

Intel CPU 2.5 GHz. Is the Speed of the Processor.

THE DIGITAL WORLD. _____

The **Smallest unit** of Information that can be transmitted is a **BIT**. A **BIT** is a Binary Number that Represents (0) **ZERO** or One (1). The BINARY Language is used by all Computers to communicate and is called <u>The Computer Language.</u> The BIT uses a **Voltage Signal** that starts from 0 (zero) and rises to 1 (one) for 1 second, then drops to Zero (0) representing **ON**/1 and **OFF**/0. <u>**Welcome to the Digital World.**</u>

<u>16 Bits is equal to:</u> **1 BYTE**

A KILO-BYTE is equal to: 1024 BYTE'S

A MEGA-BYTE is equal to: 1024 KILO-BYTE'S

A GIGA-BYTE is equal to: 1024 MEGA-BYTE'S

Kilo, Mega and Giga = Greek designators in Binary Numbers.

One KILO- METER = 1000 Meters

Difference Between MB and GB. The rate of **data** transmission in telecommunications and computer use is based on the number of bits, characters, or blocks in their systems. ... Today a byte consists of 16 bits, a kilobyte is 1024 bytes, a megabyte is 1024 kilobytes, and a **gigabyte** is 1024 megabytes.

KB, **MB**, **GB** - A kilobyte (KB) is 1,024 bytes. A megabyte (**MB**) is 1,024 kilobytes. A gigabyte (**GB**) is 1,024 megabytes. A terabyte (TB) is 1,024 gigabytes.

A bit can be 0 or 1, equivalent or off or on. ... Therefore 1KB is the same as 1024 x 8 = 8192 binary digits. Megabyte (**MB**): 1024KB equals one megabyte (**MB**). Gigabyte (**GB**): There are 1024MB in one gigabyte.

Maximum Data Transmission in Computers.

Kilobyte (1024 Bytes)

Megabyte (1024 Kilobytes)

Gigabyte (1,024 Megabytes, or 1,048,576 Kilobytes)

Terabyte (1,024 Gigabytes)

Petabyte (1,024 Terabytes, or 1,048,576 Gigabytes)

Exabyte (1,024 Petabytes)

Zettabyte (1,024 Exabytes)

Yottabyte (1,204 Zettabytes,

or 1,208,925,819,614,629,174,706,176 bytes)

History and origin of kilo, mega and more.__

The prefix *kilo* (1,000) first came into existence between 1865 and 1870. Though *mega* is used these days to mean "extremely good, great or successful," its scientific meaning is 1 million.

***Giga* comes from the Greek** word for giant, and the first use of the term is believed to have taken place at the 1947 conference of the International Union of Pure and Applied Chemistry. ***Tera* (1 trillion) comes from the Greek** word *teras* or *teratos*, meaning "marvel, monster," and has been in use since approximately 1947.

The prefixes ***exa*** (1 quintillion) and ***peta*** (1 quadrillion) were added to the International System of Units (SI) in 1975. However, the origin and history of *peta* with data measurement terms is unclear. ***Zetta*** (1 sextillion) was added to the SI metric prefixes in 1991.

When the prefixes are added to the term ***byte*,** it creates units of measurement ranging from **1,000 bytes (kilobyte) to 1 sextillion bytes (zettabyte)** of data storage capacity. **A megabyte is 1 million bytes of data storage capacity, according to the**

IBM Dictionary of Computing.

A gigabyte (GB) is equivalent to about **1 billion bytes**. There are two standards for measuring the number of bytes in a gigabyte: base-10 and base-2. Base-10 uses the decimal system to show that 1 GB equals one to the 10th power of bytes, or 1 billion bytes. <u>This is the standard most data storage manufacturers and consumers use today.</u> Computers typically use the base-2, or binary, form of measurement. Base-2 has 1 GB as equal to 1,073,741,824 bytes. The discrepancy between base-10 and base-2 measurements became more distinct as vendors began to manufacture data storage media with more capacity.

A terabyte (<u>TB</u>) is equal to approximately **1 trillion bytes,** or 1,024 GB. **A petabyte** (<u>PB</u>) is equal to two to the 50th power of bytes. There are **1,024 TB in a PB,** and about **1,024 PB equal 1 exabyte (<u>EB</u>)**. A **zettabyte** is equal to about 1,000 EB, or **1 billion TB.**

Terabyte vs. petabyte: What would it look like?

In his book, *The Singularity is Near*, futurist Raymond Kurzweil estimated **the capacity of a human being's functional memory to be 1.25 TB.** This means that the memories of 800 human beings fit into 1 PB of storage..

If the average MP3 encoding is approximately 1 MB per second (MBps), and the average song lasts about **four minutes,** then a petabyte of songs could play continuously for more than 2,000 years.

If the average smartphone camera photo is 3 MB, and the average printed photo is 8.5-inches wide, a petabyte of photos placed side by side would be more than **48,000 miles long.**

That is almost long enough to wrap around the equator twice. According to Wes Biggs, CTO at Adfonic, **1 PB can store the DNA of the entire population of the United States and then clone them twice.**

If you counted all the bits in 1 PB of storage at a rate of 1 bps, it would take **285 million years,** according to data analysts from Deloitte Analytics.

A bit is a binary digit, either a 0 or 1; a byte is eight binary digits long. If you counted 1 bps, it would take 35.7 million years.

Yottabytes and Data Storage

The future of data storage may be the **yottabyte.** It's a measure of Storage capacity equal to approximately 1,000 zettabytes, 1 trillion terabytes, a million trillion megabytes or 1 septillion bytes.

Written in decimal form, a yottabyte looks like this: 1,208,925,819,614,629,174,706,176. The prefix *yotta* is based on the

Greek letter iota. According to Paul McFedries' book *Word Spy*, it **would take 86 trillion years to download a 1 yottabyte file;** by comparison, the entire contents of the Library of Congress would equal just 10 TB.

According to a 2010 Gizmodo article, storing a yottabyte of data on terabyte-size disk drives would require 1 billion city block-size data centers, equal to combining the states of Rhode Island and Delaware.

As of late 2016, memory density had grown to the point where a yottabyte could be stored on SDX cards occupying no more than twice the size of the Hindenberg.

DR ALFONSO J. KINGLOW

COMPLETE COMPUTER TOOLS.___

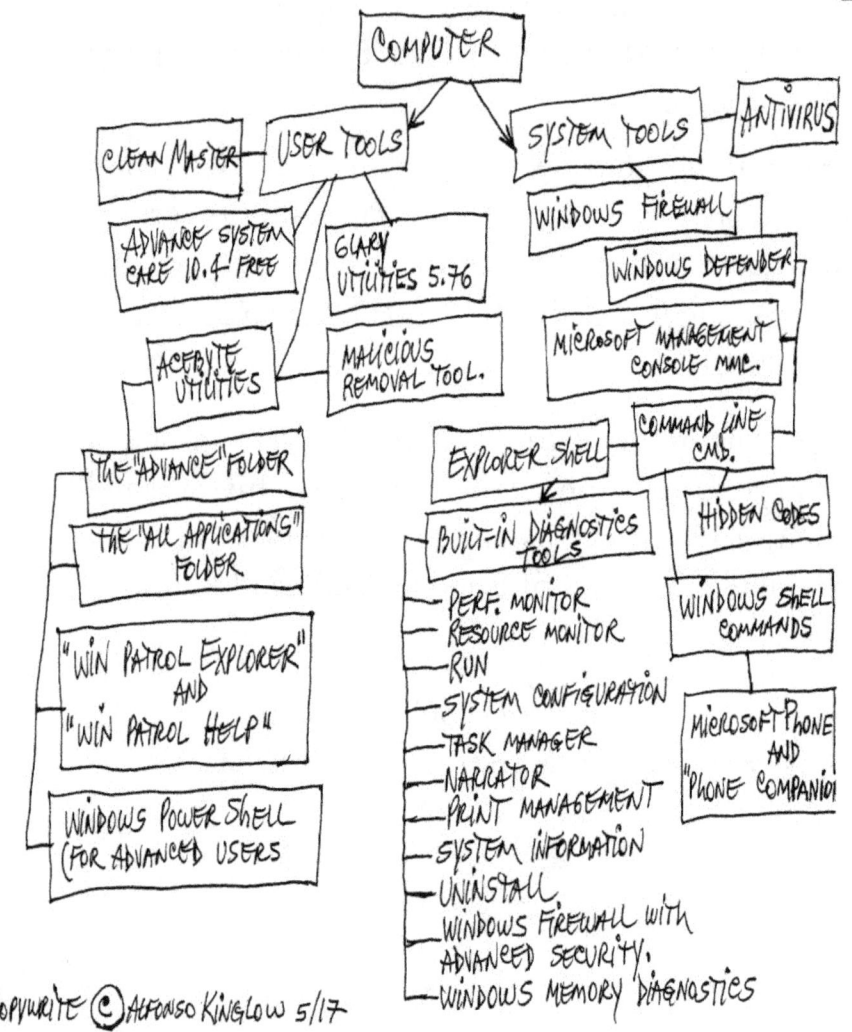

4 THE ALU ARITHMATIC LOGIC UNIT CONFIGURATIONS.

THE **ALU** IS:
Computer Hardware and Software. **The Hardware** contains the Memory, Storage and CPU, the Mouse and Keyboard and the Video Display with many internal parts like the Network Adapter and the Video Graphics Card and DVD player.

The Software is the program that runs the Computer Hardware, it is called the System Software or the Operating System. In this case the Operating System is a **GUI** (Graphic User Interface) type, called **Windows.**

International Standard Organization (ISO), International Consortium of Assigned Names and Numbers (ICANN), and FEDERAL COMMUNICATION COMISSION (FCC) and others; set the Rules and Regulations that govern Computers and how they are used.

Rules

Standards

Protocols

Computer Hardware and Software is Regulated and Organized by Rules, Standards and Protocols by **ISO, ICANN** and others..

Computer Rules: relate to the User interacting with his or her Computer. For Examples.

Turn off your Computer Correctly using **CTRL + ALT + DEL** keys together to call the Task Manager, to Log Off or **Shutdown.**

Shutdown the Standard way by selecting the Shutdown command from the Start Button.

Never press or hold down the Computer Power Button to Shutdown your Computer. Shutdown the Computer using the Windows Shutdown Software from the Start Button.

Printers

To connect a printer to the Computer, **first** Turn on the Computer and Log On; then connect the Printer via a Printer USB Cable.

Never connect a printer via Wi-Fi if the Printer is just 3 to 5 feet away from the Computer. **Always** connect the Printer via a hardwired Printer Cable with USB connector, which connects the Printer Permanently to the Computer, thus increasing the speed and output.

To prevent **eye fatigue and headaches when writing** or working on a Computer for a long period of time, like writing a document, etc...

Use **The Rule of 30.**

The RULE OF 30 APPLIES:

Look away at any object that is 30 feet away, for 30 seconds every 30 minutes.

STANDARDS

In the early 70's and 80's International Standards and National Standards were organized and established to Regulate and inform all users and Governments about the use of Computers and Frequencies assigned to Electronic devices and information devices Worldwide.

The organization was called **ISO** (International Standards Organization) from ISO many other organizations were formed, like **ICANN** (International Consortium of Assigned Name and Numbers.) That Regulates The Internet, and Computer Hardware and Software Protocols.

Local organizations were established in the USA such as **NIST** (National Institute of Science and Technology) the **FCC** (Federal Communication Commission) and others.

The Standards for Internet and Computer Networking, such as the Wi Fi Standard of **802.11 a/b/g/n** and **802.11 a/b/g/AC and AD** and the permanent Internet Cable connection Ethernet 802.3 (100 Mbps) and 1GB (Gigabit

Ethernet High Speed Network) and higher.

The **USB** (Universal Serial Buss) Standard for connecting devices to a Computer, and many more...

Graphic Standards were established for Computer Display Monitors, and LCD Displays. The most popular Standard for Pictures and Images was establish by

 JPEG (Joint Photographic Engineering Group), **GIF** (Graphic Interface Format) and others., like **PDF** (Postscript Description File) for Documents over the Internet and many more..

PROTOCOLS: A set of Rules that tell Computers how to interact with Software and Hardware, these protocols can not be changed, modified, deleted or removed.

Protocols establish how the Users interact with Computers, both hardware and software. A classic example, are the Protocols to use the Internet.

 The Protocol: **HTTP** (Hypertext Transport Protocol) and the **URL** (Universal Resource Locator) and the **WWW** (World Wide Web) the HP Printer Protocols;

like **HPDL, HPGL, HPIB,** (HP Description Language, HP Graphic Language, HP Interface Buss) used Worldwide and established by Hewlett Packard Company. Understanding how Protocols work and why Computers have to comply with these established Protocols will help the user better understand that Computers are TASK DRIVEN MACHINES that follow a set of Rules and

Protocols. If the Users know how the Rules and Protocols work in Hardware and Software, it will become easy to understand how Computers work, and can help us to be more Productive.

NEW WI-FI STANDARD.

The New Wi-Fi Standard That Will Make the 802.11AC Obsolete.

The first wave of 802.11ac routers currently available on the market are based on earlier drafts of the 802.11ac standard and will no longer be the fastest standard on the market. The second wave of 802.11ac devices are based on the final ratified standard and are set to include new features that better optimize wireless networks.

802.11AC Standard: Wave 1 vs. Wave 2

802.11ac Wave 2 is set to include MU-MIMO capabilities among other advances that will give routers a speed boost from the original 3.47 Gbps in first generation to 6.93 Gbps in the final iteration of the standard.

MU-MIMO or Multiple-user multiple input/multiple output "enables [routers] to send multiple spatial streams to multiple clients simultaneously". With 160 MHz channel bonding (as opposed to 80 Mhz bonding over wave 1) and backwards compatibility with previous standards, the new standard boasts a performance boost over the first generation of 802.11ac routers. With a physical link rate of nearly 7 Gbps, users hoping to upgrade to 802.11ac <u>should consider waiting to catch the second wave.</u>

Market Trends

Dell'Oro Group has published a report that notes that the "Wireless LAN (WLAN) market grew eight percent in the third quarter 2014 versus the yearago period" and that

> "Enterprise-class 802.11ac-based radio access points grew a robust 40 percent versus the second quarter 2014."

> The report forecasts that the WLAN market will be stimulated with the release of 802.11ac Wave 2 equipment along with government funding in the US meant to support wireless connectivity in schools and libraries.

The New Standard 802.11ax

But even the second generation of the 802.11ac standard cannot compare with the wireless speeds of a still newer specification. The 802.11ax standard is set to "not just increase the overall speed of a network"but to "quadruple wireless speeds of

individual clients." Huawei's research and development labs , have reported to successfully reach wireless connections speeds of 10 Gbps utilizing the 5GHz frequency band.

The standard is set to be finalized in 2019, but manufacturers can be expected to release products based on the pre-standard as early as 2018.

While wireless connections keep getting faster, the options for internet users to connect to the internet keep expanding. In the near future, users can be expected to connect to the internet using LED lights, or gain wireless access to the internet by connecting to a micro-satellite orbiting the Earth.

What Will 802.11ax Bring To Your Airspace?

MORE ABOUT THE NEW **WIRELESS STANDARD 802.11AX FOR 2020.**

The industry is on the cusp of a new wireless protocol. It's been almost ten years since 802.11ac was proposed, and five years since final ratification. 802.11ac has been built upon to deliver speeds past 1 Gpbs and has become the preferred method of wireless connectivity for computers and mobile devices alike.

However, 802.11ac exposes many of the problems we have with Wi-Fi coverage that is just *faster*. As Wi-Fi has become the primary method of connectivity for a range of devices we've seen how the protocol breaks down under certain conditions. We've seen how the accumulation of little issues can keep our speeds down and how simply making things bigger and faster won't fix them. That's why 802.11ax is taking a much firmer hand in directing wireless traffic.

One of the biggest changes in **802.11ax** is the addition of Orthogonal Frequency-Division Multiple Access (OFDMA). That's a fancy acronym that describes the way that 802.11ax handles sub-channel communications. We've seen that the explosion of wireless devices in the past years has meant that there are many, many more devices trying to talk to the an access point (AP) at any one given time. This means that there are a lot of clients waiting in line to deliver and receive data.

In 802.11ac and earlier protocols any transmission has to use the entire channel to transmit or receive.

That doesn't mean much if you have a relatively skinny 20 MHz channel width. But if you've cranked the radio all the way up to 160 MHz, you're sending 8 times the data but still using the entire channel nomatter the size of the packet. This is inefficient and wastes valuable time that could be used by other clients.

802.11ax changes things by dividing those channels into a collection of subchannels. This allows data to be transmitted in parallel across a series of smaller channels instead of taking an entire wide channel for small things like acknowledgment (ACK) frames and such. For small packets, this means that a client can transmit and only use the necessary amount of bandwidth for their frame. This means they get off the air faster and can let the AP utilize those other sub channels for other clients.

For larger packet sizes, splitting things into a group of parallel transmissions saves transmission times versus sequential transmission. Research indicates that this could be up to three times faster for simple parallel versus sequential transmission. An increase in speed of 3x is nothing to sneeze at!

The best part is that these changes are in both the 5 GHz and 2.4 GHz spectrum. 802.11ac focused only on 5 GHz and left users of the older 2.4 GHz spectrum out in the cold. With 802.11ax, we're going to see improvements across the board. Much like the older 802.11n standard, even clients that don't support 802.11 ax should see an improvement thanks to better handling of transmission and such.

New Standards are emerging even during a Pandemic like the one we are now experiencing in 2020 and 2021, but Technology moves forward.

The new Wi-Fi Standards will give us the speed that we need to move forward in Technology.

5 CLEANING TOOLS

These are the Free Cleaning Tools that every User should have on their Computers:

1. ADVANCE SYSTEM CARE vers 14.4
2. GLARY UTILITIES vers 5.165
3. CLEAN MASTER vers 6.6
4. SMART DEFRAG vers 6.7
5. ACEBYTE UTILITIES vers 3.0
6. AVG ANTIVIRUS FREE
7. ADVANCE FOLDER created with the hidden Code., presented in this book.

Advance System Care is the main primary tool that should be run once a week to keep the computer clean and with top performance.

Clean Master should be run every 3 days to clean junk and other malware from the Computer.

Smart Defrag is a Hard Disk defragmenter that will clean up broken and fragmented files on the hard drive and save space for Storage making the HD to run faster.

Glary Utilities should be run every week to clean Junk in the system files to speed up the CPU process.

AVG Antivirus install it and it will automatic protect the Computer from Viruses.

Advance Folder will show you how to fix ANY problems

with Windows 10 Computer it contains 175 files.

Acebyte Utilities should be run every week to clean up both system and hardware junk that can slow down the computer.

The **DXDIAG.EXE** Diagnostic Tool can be run at any time to analyze and troubleshoot any problem the computer may have at Startup. Run it by typing in the start window:

DXDIAG.EXE or Copy the Application to the Desktop.

6 BASIC COMPUTER GLOSSARY

SENIORS BASIC COMPUTER GLOSSARY.

One of the earliest operating systems was **MS-DOS,** developed by Microsoft for IBM PC. It was a **Command Line Interface (CLI)** OS that revolutionized the PC market. **DOS** was difficult to use because of its interface. The users needed to remember instructions to do their tasks. To make computers more accessible and user-friendly, Microsoft developed **Graphical User Interface (GUI)** based OS called **Windows**, which transformed the way people used computers.

THE BASIC COMPUTER GLOSSARY

Updated. (**Different from Basic Computer Terms and Acronyms.**)

Applet

A small Java application that is downloaded by an ActiveX or Java-enabled web browser. Once it has been downloaded, the applet will run on the user's computer. Common applets include financial calculators and web drawing programs.

Application

Computer software that performs a task or set of tasks, such as word processing or drawing. Applications are also referred to as programs.

ASCII

American Standard Code for Information Interchange, an encoding system for converting keyboard characters and instructions into the binary number code that the computer understands.

Bandwidth

The capacity of a networked connection. Bandwidth determines how much data can be sent along the networked wires. Bandwidth is particularly important for Internet connections, since greater bandwidth also means faster downloads.

Binary code

The most basic language a computer understands, it is composed of a series of 0s and 1s. The computer interprets the code to form numbers, letters, punctuation marks, and symbols.

Bit

The smallest piece of computer information, either the number 0 or 1. In short they are called binary digits.

Boot

To start up a computer. Cold boot means restarting computer after the power is turned off. Warm boot means restarting computer without turning off the power.

Browser

Software used to navigate the Internet. Google Chrome, Firefox, Netscape Navigator and Microsoft Internet Explorer are today's most popular browsers for accessing the World Wide Web.

Bug

A malfunction due to an error in the program or a defect in the equipment.

Byte

Most computers use combinations of eight bits, called bytes, to represent one character of data or instructions. For example, the word **cat** has three characters, and it would be represented by three bytes.

Cache

A small data-memory storage area that a computer can use to instantly re-access data instead of re-reading the data from the original source, such as a hard drive. Browsers use a cache to store web pages so that the user may view them again without reconnecting to the Web.

CAD-CAM

Computer Aided Drawing - Computer Aided Manufacturing. The instructions stored in a computer that will be translated to very precise operating instructions to a robot, such as for assembling cars or laser-cutting signage.

CD-ROM

Compact Disc Read-Only Memory, an optically read disc designed to hold information such as music, reference materials, or computer software. A single CD-ROM can hold around 640 megabytes of data, enough for several encyclopaedias. Most software programs are now delivered on CD-ROMs.

CGI

Common Gateway Interface, a programming standard that allows visitors to fill out form fields on a Web page and have that information interact with a database, possibly coming back to the user as

another Web page. CGI may also refer to Computer-Generated Imaging, the process in which sophisticated computer programs create still and animated graphics, such as special effects for movies.

Chat

Typing text into a message box on a screen to engage in dialogue with one or more people via the Internet or other network.

Chip

A tiny wafer of silicon containing miniature electric circuits that can store millions of bits of information.

Client

A single user of a network application that is operated from a server. A client/server architecture allows many people to use the same data simultaneously. The program's main component (the data) resides on a centralized server, with smaller components (user interface) on each client.

Cookie

A text file sent by a Web server that is stored on the hard drive of a computer and relays back to the Web server things about the user, his or her computer, and/or his or her computer activities.

CPU

Central Processing Unit. The brain of the computer.

Cracker

A person who breaks in to a computer through a network, without authorization and with mischievous or destructive intent.

Crash

A hardware or software problem that causes information to be lost or the computer to malfunction. Sometimes a crash can cause permanent damage to a computer.

Cursor

A moving position-indicator displayed on a computer monitor that shows a computer operator where the next action or operation will take place.

Cyberspace

Slang for internet ie. An international conglomeration of interconnected computer networks. Begun in the late 1960s, it was developed in the 1970s to allow government and university researchers to share information. The Internet is not controlled by any single group or organization. Its original focus was research and communications, but it continues to expand, offering a wide array of resources for business and home users.

Database

A collection of similar information stored in a file, such as a database of addresses. This information may be created and stored in a database management system (DBMS).

Debug

Slang. To find and correct equipment defects or program malfunctions.

Default

The pre-defined configuration of a system or an application. In most programs, the defaults can be changed to reflect personal preferences.

Desktop

The main directory of the user interface. Desktops usually contain icons that represent links to the hard drive, a network (if there is one), and a trash or recycling can for files to be deleted. It can also display icons of frequently used applications, as requested by the user.

Desktop publishing

The production of publication-quality documents using a personal computer in combination with text, graphics, and page layout programs.

Directory

A repository where all files are kept on computer.

Disk

Two distinct types. The names refer to the media inside the container:

A hard disc stores vast amounts of data. It is usually inside the computer but can be a separate peripheral on the outside. Hard discs are made up of several rigid coated metal discs. Currently, hard discs can store 15 to 30 Gb (gigabytes).

A floppy disc, 3.5" square, usually inserted into the computer and can store about 1.4 megabytes of data. The 3.5" square floppies have a very thin, flexible disc inside. There is also an intermediate-sized floppy disc, trademarked Zip discs, which can store 250 megabytes of data.

Disk drive

The equipment that operates a hard or floppy disc.

Domain

Represents an IP (Internet Protocol) address or set of IP addresses that comprise a domain. The domain name appears in URLs to identify web pages or in email addresses. For example, the email address for the First Lady is first.lady@whitehouse.gov, whitehouse.gov, being the domain name. Each domain name ends with a suffix that indicates what top level domain it belongs to. These are : .com for commercial, .gov for government, .org for organization, .edu for educational institution, .biz for business, .info for information, .tv for television, .ws for website. Domain suffixes may also indicate the country in which the domain is registered. No two parties can ever hold the same domain name.

Domain name

The name of a network or computer linked to the Internet. Domains are defined by a common IP address or set of similar IP (Internet Protocol) addresses.

Download

The process of transferring information from a web site (or other remote location on a network) to the computer. It is possible to download a file which include text, image, audio, video and many others.

DOS

Disk Operating System. An operating system designed for early IBM-compatible PCs.

Drop-down menu

A menu window that opens vertically on-screen to display context-related options. Also called pop-up menu or pull-down menu.

DSL

Digital Subscriber Line, a method of connecting to the Internet via a phone line. A DSL connection uses copper telephone lines but is able to relay data at much higher speeds than modems and does not interfere with telephone use.

DVD

Digital Video Disc. Similar to a CD-ROM, it stores and plays both audio and video.

E-book

An electronic (usually hand-held) reading device that allows a person to view digitally stored reading materials.

Email

Electronic mail; messages, including memos or letters, sent electronically between networked computers that may be across the office or around the world.

Emoticon

A text-based expression of emotion created from ASCII characters that mimics a facial expression when viewed with your head tilted to the left. Here are some examples:

Smiling
Frowning
Winking

Crying

Encryption

The process of transmitting scrambled data so that only authorized recipients can unscramble it. For instance, encryption is used to scramble credit card information when purchases are made over the Internet.

Ethernet

A type of network.

Ethernet card

A board inside a computer to which a network cable can be attached.

File

A set of data that is stored in the computer.

Firewall

A set of security programs that protect a computer from outside interference or access via the Internet.

Folder

A structure for containing electronic files. In some operating systems, it is called a directory.

Fonts

Sets of typefaces (or characters) that come in

different styles and sizes.

Freeware

Software created by people who are willing to give it away for the satisfaction of sharing or knowing they helped to simplify other people's lives. It may be free-standing software, or it may add functionality to existing software.

FTP

File Transfer Protocol, a format and set of rules for transferring files from a host to a remote computer.

Gigabyte (GB)

1024 megabytes. Also called gig.

Glitch

The cause of an unexpected malfunction.

Gopher

An Internet search tool that allows users to access textual information through a series of menus, or if using FTP, through downloads.

GUI

Graphical User Interface, a system that simplifies

selecting computer commands by enabling the user to point to symbols or illustrations (called icons) on the computer screen with a mouse.

Groupware

Software that allows networked individuals to form groups and collaborate on documents, programs, or databases.

Hacker

A person with technical expertise who experiments with computer systems to determine how to develop additional features. Hackers are occasionally requested by system administrators to try and break into systems via a network to test security. The term hacker is sometimes incorrectly used interchangeably with cracker. A hacker is called a white hat and a cracker a black hat.

Hard copy

A paper printout of what you have prepared on the computer.

Hard drive

Another name for the hard disc that stores information in a computer.

Hardware

The physical and mechanical components of a computer system, such as the electronic circuitry, chips, monitor, disks, disk drives, keyboard, modem, and printer.

Home page

The main page of a Web site used to greet visitors, provide information about the site, or to direct the viewer to other pages on the site.

HTML

Hypertext Markup Language, a standard of text markup conventions used for documents on the World Wide Web. Browsers interpret the codes to give the text structure and formatting (such as bold, blue, or italic).

HTTP

Hypertext Transfer Protocol, a common system used to request and send HTML documents on the World Wide Web. It is the first portion of all URL addresses on the World Wide Web.

HTTPS

Hypertext Transfer Protocol Secure, often used in intracompany internet sites. Passwords are required to gain access.

Hyperlink

Text or an image that is connected by hypertext coding to a different location. By selecting the text or image with a mouse, the computer jumps to (or displays) the linked text.

Hypermedia

Integrates audio, graphics, and/or video through links embedded in the main program.

Hypertext

A system for organizing text through links, as opposed to a menu-driven hierarchy such as Gopher. Most Web pages include hypertext links to other pages at that site, or to other sites on the World Wide Web.Icons

Symbols or illustrations appearing on the computer screen that indicate program files or other computer functions.

Input

Data that goes into a computer device.

Input device

A device, such as a keyboard, stylus and tablet,

mouse, puck, or microphone, that allows input of information (letters, numbers, sound, video) to a computer.

Instant messaging (IM)

A chat application that allows two or more people to communicate over the Internet via real-time keyed-in messages.

Interface

The interconnections that allow a device, a program, or a person to interact. Hardware interfaces are the cables that connect the device to its power source and to other devices. Software interfaces allow the program to communicate with other programs (such as the operating system), and user interfaces allow the user to communicate with the program (e.g., via mouse, menu commands, icons, voice commands, etc.).

Internet

An international conglomeration of interconnected computer networks. Begun in the late 1960s, it was developed in the 1970s to allow government and university researchers to share information. The Internet is not controlled by any single group or organization. Its original focus was research and communications, but it continues to expand, offering a wide array of resources for business and home users.

IP (Internet Protocol) address

An Internet Protocol address is a unique set of numbers used to locate another computer on a network. The format of an IP address is a 32-bit string of four numbers separated by periods. Each number can be from 0 to 255 (i.e., 1.154.10.255). Within a closed network IP addresses may be assigned at random, however, IP addresses of web servers must be registered to avoid duplicates.

Java

An object-oriented programming language designed specifically for programs (particularly multimedia) to be used over the Internet. Java allows programmers to create small programs or applications (applets) to enhance Web sites.

JavaScript/ECMA script

A programming language used almost exclusively to manipulate content on a web page. Common JavaScript functions include validating forms on a web page, creating dynamic page navigation menus, and image rollovers.

Kilobyte (K or KB)

Equal to 1,024 bytes.

Linux

A UNIX - like, open-source operating system developed primarily by Linus Torvalds. Linux is free and runs on many platforms, including both PCs and Macintoshes. Linux is an open-source operating system, meaning that the source code of the operating system is freely available to the public. Programmers may redistribute and modify the code, as long as they don't collect royalties on their work or deny access to their code. Since development is not restricted to a single corporation more programmers can debug and improve the source code faster.

Laptop and notebook

Small, lightweight, portable battery-powered computers that can fit onto your lap. They each have a thin, flat, liquid crystal display screen.

Macro

A script that operates a series of commands to perform a function. It is set up to automate repetitive tasks.

Mac OS

An operating system with a graphical user interface, developed by Apple for Macintosh computers. Current System X.1.(10) combines the traditional Mac interface with a strong underlying UNIX. Operating system for increased performance and stability.

Megabyte (MB)

Equal to 1,048,576 bytes, usually rounded off to one million bytes (also called a meg).

Memory

Temporary storage for information, including applications and documents. The information must be stored to a permanent device, such as a hard disc or CD-ROM before the power is turned off, or the information will be lost. Computer memory is measured in terms of the amount of information it can store, commonly in megabytes or gigabytes.

Menu

A context-related list of options that users can choose from.

Menu bar

The horizontal strip across the top of an

application's window. Each word on the strip has a context sensitive drop-down menu containing features and actions that are available for the application in use.

Merge

To combine two or more files into a single file.

MHz

An abbreviation for **Megahertz, or one million hertz.** One MHz represents one million clock cycles per second and is the measure of a computer microprocessor's speed. For example, a microprocessor that runs at 300 MHz executes 300 million cycles per second. Each instruction a computer receives takes a fixed number of clock cycles to carry out, therefore the more cycles a computer can execute per second, the faster its programs run. Megahertz is also a unit of measure for bandwidth.

Microprocessor

A complete central processing unit (CPU) contained on a single silicon chip.

Minimize

A term used in a GUI operating system that uses windows. It refers to reducing a window to an icon, or a label at the bottom of the screen, allowing another window to be viewed.

Modem

A device that connects two computers together over a telephone or cable line by converting the computer's data into an audio signal. Modem is a contraction for the process it performs : modulate-demodulate.

Monitor

A video display terminal.

Mouse

A small hand-held device, similar to a trackball, used to control the position of the cursor on the video display; movements of the mouse on a desktop correspond to movements of the cursor on the screen.

MP3

Compact audio and video file format. The small size of the files makes them easy to download and e-mail. Format used in portable playback devices.

Multimedia

Software programs that combine text and graphics with sound, video, and animation. A multimedia PC contains the hardware to support these capabilities.

MS-DOS

An early operating system developed by Microsoft Corporation (Microsoft Disc Operating System).

Network

A system of interconnected computers.

Open source

Computer programs whose original source code was revealed to the general public so that it could be developed openly. Software licensed as open source can be freely changed or adapted to new uses, meaning that the source code of the operating system is freely available to the public. Programmers may redistribute and modify the code, as long as they don't collect royalties on their work or deny access to their code. Since development is not restricted to a single corporation more programmers can debug and improve the source code faster.

Operating system

A set of instructions that tell a computer on how to operate when it is turned on. It sets up a filing system to store files and tells the computer how to display information on a video display. Most PC operating systems are DOS (disc operated system) systems, meaning the instructions are stored on a disc (as opposed to being originally stored in the microprocessors of the computer). Other well-known operating systems include UNIX, Linux, Macintosh, and Windows.

Output

Data that come out of a computer device. For example, information displayed on the monitor, sound from the speakers, and information printed to paper.

Palm

A hand-held computer.

PC

Personal computer. Generally refers to computers running Windows with a Pentium processor.

PC board

Printed Circuit board, a board printed or etched with a circuit and processors. Power supplies, information storage devices, or changers are attached.

PDA

Personal Digital Assistant, a hand-held computer that can store daily appointments, phone numbers, addresses, and other important information. Most PDAs link to a desktop or laptop computer to download or upload information.

PDF

Portable Document Format, a format presented by Adobe Acrobat that allows documents to be shared over a variety of operating systems. Documents can contain words and pictures and be formatted to have electronic links to other parts of the document or to places on the web.

Pentium chip

Intel's fifth generation of sophisticated high-speed microprocessors. Pentium means the fifth element.

Peripheral

Any external device attached to a computer to enhance operation. Examples include external hard drive, scanner, printer, speakers, keyboard, mouse, trackball, stylus and tablet, and joystick.

Personal computer (PC)

A single-user computer containing a central processing unit (CPU) and one or more memory circuits.

Petabyte

A measure of memory or storage capacity and is approximately a thousand terabytes.

Petaflop

A theoretical measure of a computer's speed and can be expressed as a thousand-trillion floating-point operations per second.

Platform

The operating system, such as UNIX, Macintosh, Windows, on which a computer is based.

Plug and play

Computer hardware or peripherals that come set up with necessary software so that when attached to a computer, they are recognized by the computer and are ready to use.

Pop-up menu

A menu window that opens vertically or horizontally on-screen to display context-related options. Also called drop-down menu or pull-down menu.

Power PC

A competitor of the Pentium chip. It is a new generation of powerful sophisticated microprocessors produced from an Apple-IBM-Motorola alliance.

Printer

A mechanical device for printing a computer's output on paper. There are three major types of printer:

> **Dot matrix** - creates individual letters, made up of a series of tiny ink dots, by punching a ribbon with the ends of tiny wires. (This type of printer is most often used in industrial settings, such as direct mail for labelling.)
>
> **Ink jet** - sprays tiny droplets of ink particles onto paper.
>
> **Laser** - uses a beam of light to reproduce the image of each page using a magnetic charge that attracts dry toner that is transferred to paper and sealed with heat.

Program

A precise series of instructions written in a computer language that tells the computer what to do and how to do it. Programs are also called software or applications.

Programming language

A series of instructions written by a programmer according to a given set of rules or conventions (syntax). High-level programming languages are independent of the device on which the application (or program) will eventually run; low-level languages are specific to each program or platform. Programming language instructions are converted into programs in language specific to a particular machine or operating system (machine language). So that the computer can interpret and carry out the instructions. Some common programming languages are BASIC, C, C++, dBASE, FORTRAN, and Perl.

Puck

An input device, like a mouse. It has a magnifying glass with crosshairs on the front of it that allows the operator to position it precisely when tracing a drawing for use with CAD-CAM software.

Pull-down menu

A menu window that opens vertically on-screen to display context-related options. Also called drop-down menu or pop-up menu.

Push technology

Internet tool that delivers specific information directly to a user's desktop, eliminating the need to surf for it. PointCast, which delivers news in user-defined categories, is a popular example of this technology.

QuickTime

Audio-visual software that allows movie-delivery via the Internet and e-mail. QuickTime images are viewed on a monitor.

RAID

Redundant Array of Inexpensive Disks, a method of spreading information across several disks set up to act as a unit, using two different techniques:

- **Disk striping** - storing a bit of information across several discs (instead of storing it all on one disc and hoping that the disc doesn't crash).

- **Disk mirroring** - simultaneously storing a copy of information on another disc so that the information can be recovered if the main disc crashes.

RAM

Random Access Memory, one of two basic types of memory. Portions of programs are stored in RAM when the program is launched so that the program will run faster. Though a PC has a fixed amount of RAM, only portions of it will be accessed by the computer at any given time. Also called memory.

Right-click

Using the right mouse button to open context-sensitive drop-down menus.

ROM

Read-Only Memory, one of two basic types of memory. ROM contains only permanent information put there by the manufacturer. Information in ROM cannot be altered, nor can the memory be dynamically allocated by the computer or its operator.

Scanner

An electronic device that uses light-sensing equipment to scan paper images such as text, photos, and illustrations and translate the images into signals that the computer can then store, modify, or distribute.

Search engine

Software that makes it possible to look for and retrieve material on the Internet, particularly the Web. Some popular search engines are Alta Vista, Google, HotBot, Yahoo!, Web Crawler, and Lycos.

Server

A computer that shares its resources and

information with other computers, called clients, on a network.

Shareware

Software created by people who are willing to sell it at low cost or no cost for the gratification of sharing. It may be freestanding software, or it may add functionality to existing software.

Software

Computer programs; also called applications.

Spider

A process search engines use to investigate new pages on a web site and collect the information that needs to be put in their indices.

Spreadsheet

Software that allows one to calculate numbers in a format that is similar to pages in a conventional ledger.

Storage

Devices used to store massive amounts of information so that it can be readily retrieved. Devices include RAIDs, CD-ROMs, DVDs.

Streaming

Taking packets of information (sound or visual) from the Internet and storing it in temporary files to allow it to play in continuous flow.

Stylus and tablet

An input device similar to a mouse. The stylus is pen shaped. It is used to draw on a tablet (like drawing on paper) and the tablet transfers the information to the computer. The tablet responds to pressure. The firmer the pressure used to draw, the thicker the line appears.

Surfing

Exploring the Internet.

Surge protector

A controller to protect the computer and make up for variances in voltage.

Telnet

A way to communicate with a remote computer over a network.

Trackball

Input device that controls the position of the cursor on the screen; the unit is mounted near the keyboard, and movement is controlled by moving a ball.

Terabytes (TB)

A thousand gigabytes.

Teraflop

A measure of a computer's speed. It can be expressed as a trillion floating-point operations per second.

Trojan Horse

See virus.

UNIX

A very powerful operating system used as the basis of many high-end computer applications.

Upload

The process of transferring information from a computer to a web site (or other remote location on a network). To transfer information from a computer to a web site (or other remote location on a network).

URL

Uniform Resource Locator.

The protocol for identifying a document on the Web.

A Web address (e.g., www.tutorialspoint.com). A URL is unique to each user. See also domain.

UPS

Universal Power Supply or Uninterruptible Power Supply. An electrical power supply that includes a battery to provide enough power to a computer during an outage to back-up data and properly shut down.

USB

A multiple-socket USB connector that allows several USB-compatible devices to be connected to a computer.

USENET

A large unmoderated and unedited bulletin board on the Internet that offers thousands of forums, called newsgroups. These range from newsgroups exchanging information on scientific advances to celebrity fan clubs.

User friendly

A program or device whose use is intuitive to people with a non-technical background.

Video teleconferencing

A remote "face-to-face chat," when two or more people using a webcam and an Internet telephone connection chat online. The webcam enables both live voice and video.

Virtual reality (VR)

A technology that allows one to experience and interact with images in a simulated three-dimensional environment. For example, you could design a room in a house on your computer and actually feel that you are walking around in it even though it was never built. (The Holodeck in the science-fiction TV series Star Trek : Voyager would be the ultimate virtual reality.) Current technology requires the user to wear a special helmet, viewing goggles, gloves, and other equipment that transmits and receives information from the computer.

Virus

An unauthorized piece of computer code attached to a computer program or portions of a computer system that secretly copies itself from one computer to another by shared discs and over telephone and cable lines. It can destroy information stored on the computer, and in extreme cases, can destroy operability. Computers can be protected from viruses if the operator utilizes good virus prevention software and keeps the virus definitions up to date. Most viruses are not programmed to spread themselves. They have to be sent to another computer by e-mail, sharing, or applications. The worm is an exception, because it is programmed to replicate itself by sending copies to other computers listed in the e-mail address book in the computer. There are many kinds of viruses, for example:

- Boot viruses place some of their code in the start-up disk sector to automatically execute when booting. Therefore, when an infected machine boots, the virus loads and runs.

- File viruses attached to program files (files with the extension .exe). When you run the infected program, the virus code executes.

- Macro viruses copy their macros to templates and/or other application document files.

- Trojan Horse is a malicious, security-breaking program that is disguised as something being such as a screen saver or game.

- Worm launches an application that destroys information on your hard drive. It also sends a copy of the virus to everyone in the computer's e-mail address book.

WAV

A sound format (pronounced wave) used to reproduce sounds on a computer.

Webcam

A video camera/computer setup that takes live images and sends them to a Web browser.

Window

A portion of a computer display used in a graphical interface that enables users to select commands by pointing to illustrations or symbols with a mouse. "Windows" is also the name Microsoft adopted for its popular operating system.

World Wide Web ("WWW" or "the Web")

A network of servers on the Internet that use hypertext-linked databases and files. It was developed in 1989 by Tim Berners-Lee, a British computer scientist, and is now the primary platform of the Internet. The feature that distinguishes the Web from other Internet applications is its ability to display graphics in addition to text.

Word processor

A computer system or program for setting, editing, revising, correcting, storing, and printing text.

WYSIWYG

What You See Is What You Get. When using most word processors, page layout programs (See desktop publishing), and web page design programs, words and images will be displayed on the monitor as they will look on the printed page or web page.

<u>Basic Computer Glossary</u>, different from <u>Basic Computer Terms.</u>

Applet

A small Java application that is downloaded by an ActiveX or Java-enabled web browser. Once it has been downloaded, the applet will run on the user's computer. Common applets include financial calculators and web drawing programs.

Application

Computer software that performs a task or set of tasks, such as word processing or drawing. Applications are also referred to as programs.

ASCII

American Standard Code for Information Interchange, an encoding system for converting keyboard characters and instructions into the binary number code that the computer understands.

Bandwidth

The capacity of a networked connection. Bandwidth determines how much data can be sent along the networked wires. Bandwidth is particularly important for Internet connections, since greater bandwidth also means faster downloads.

Binary code

The most basic language a computer understands, it is composed of a series of 0s and 1s. The computer interprets the code to form numbers, letters, punctuation marks, and symbols.

Bit

The smallest piece of computer information, either the number 0 or 1. In short they are called binary digits.

Boot

To start up a computer. Cold boot means restarting computer after the power is turned off. Warm boot means restarting computer without turning off the power.

Browser

Software used to navigate the Internet. Google Chrome, Firefox, Netscape Navigator and Microsoft Internet Explorer are today's most popular browsers for accessing the World Wide Web.

Bug

A malfunction due to an error in the program or a defect in the equipment.

Byte

Most computers use combinations of eight bits, called bytes, to represent one character of data or instructions. For example, the word **cat** has three characters, and it would be represented by three bytes.

Cache

A small data-memory storage area that a computer can use to instantly re-access data instead of re-reading the data from the original source, such as a hard drive. Browsers use a cache to store web pages so that the user may view them again without reconnecting to the Web.

CAD-CAM

Computer Aided Drawing - Computer Aided Manufacturing. The instructions stored in a computer that will be translated to very precise operating instructions to a robot, such as for assembling cars or laser-cutting signage.

CD-ROM

Compact Disc Read-Only Memory, an optically read disc designed to hold information such as music, reference materials, or computer software. A single CD-ROM can hold around 640 megabytes of data, enough for several encyclopaedias. Most software programs are now delivered on CD-ROMs.

CGI

Common Gateway Interface, a programming standard that allows visitors to fill out form fields on a Web page and have that information interact with a database, possibly coming back to the user as another Web page. CGI may also refer to Computer-Generated Imaging, the process in which sophisticated computer programs create still and animated graphics, such as special effects for movies.

Chat

Typing text into a message box on a screen to engage in dialogue with one or more people via the Internet or other network.

Chip

A tiny wafer of silicon containing miniature electric circuits that can store millions of bits of information.

Client

A single user of a network application that is operated from a server. A client/server architecture allows many people to use the same data simultaneously. The program's main component (the data) resides on a centralized server, with smaller components (user interface) on each client.

Cookie

A text file sent by a Web server that is stored on the hard drive of a computer and relays back to the Web server things about the user, his or her computer, and/or his or her computer activities.

CPU

Central Processing Unit. The brain of the computer.

Cracker

A person who breaks in to a computer through a network, without authorization and with mischievous or destructive intent.

Crash

A hardware or software problem that causes information to be lost or the computer to malfunction. Sometimes a crash can cause permanent damage to a computer.

Cursor

A moving position-indicator displayed on a computer monitor that shows a computer operator where the next action or operation will take place.

Cyberspace

Slang for internet ie. An international conglomeration of interconnected computer networks. Begun in the late 1960s, it was developed in the 1970s to allow government and university researchers to share information. The Internet is not controlled by any single group or organization. Its original focus was research and communications, but it continues to expand, offering a wide array of resources for business and home users.

Database

A collection of similar information stored in a file, such as a database of addresses. This information may be created and stored in a database management system (DBMS).

Debug

Slang. To find and correct equipment defects or program malfunctions.

Default

The pre-defined configuration of a system or an application. In most programs, the defaults can be changed to reflect personal preferences.

Desktop

The main directory of the user interface. Desktops usually contain icons that represent links to the hard drive, a network (if there is one), and a trash or recycling can for files to be deleted. It can also display icons of frequently used applications, as requested by the user.

Desktop publishing

The production of publication-quality documents using a personal computer in combination with text, graphics, and page layout programs.

Directory

A repository where all files are kept on computer.

Disk

Two distinct types. The names refer to the media inside the container:

A hard disc stores vast amounts of data. It is usually inside the computer but can be a separate peripheral on the outside. Hard discs are made up of several rigid coated metal discs. Currently, hard discs can store 15 to 30 Gb (gigabytes).

A floppy disc, 3.5" square, usually inserted into the computer and can store about 1.4 megabytes of data. The 3.5" square floppies have a very thin, flexible disc inside. There is also an intermediate-sized floppy disc, trademarked Zip discs, which can store 250 megabytes of data.

Disk drive

The equipment that operates a hard or floppy disc.

Domain

Represents an IP (Internet Protocol) address or set

of IP addresses that comprise a domain. The domain name appears in URLs to identify web pages or in email addresses. For example, the email address for the First Lady is first.lady@whitehouse.gov, whitehouse.gov, being the domain name. Each domain name ends with a suffix that indicates what top level domain it belongs to. These are : .com for commercial, .gov for government, .org for organization, .edu for educational institution, .biz for business, .info for information, .tv for television, .ws for website. Domain suffixes may also indicate the country in which the domain is registered. No two parties can ever hold the same domain name.

Domain name

The name of a network or computer linked to the Internet. Domains are defined by a common IP address or set of similar IP (Internet Protocol) addresses.

Download

The process of transferring information from a web site (or other remote location on a network) to the computer. It is possible to download a file which include text, image, audio, video and many others.

DOS

Disk Operating System. An operating system

designed for early IBM-compatible PCs.

Drop-down menu

A menu window that opens vertically on-screen to display context-related options. Also called pop-up menu or pull-down menu.

DSL

Digital Subscriber Line, a method of connecting to the Internet via a phone line. A DSL connection uses copper telephone lines but is able to relay data at much higher speeds than modems and does not interfere with telephone use.

DVD

Digital Video Disc. Similar to a CD-ROM, it stores and plays both audio and video.

E-book

An electronic (usually hand-held) reading device that allows a person to view digitally stored reading materials.

Email

Electronic mail; messages, including memos or letters, sent electronically between networked computers that may be across the office or around the world.

Emoticon

A text-based expression of emotion created from ASCII characters that mimics a facial expression when viewed with your head tilted to the left. Here are some examples:

> Smiling
> Frowning
> Winking
>
> Crying

Encryption

The process of transmitting scrambled data so that only authorized recipients can unscramble it. For instance, encryption is used to scramble credit card information when purchases are made over the Internet.

Ethernet

A type of network.

Ethernet card

A board inside a computer to which a network cable can be attached.

File

A set of data that is stored in the computer.

Firewall

A set of security programs that protect a computer from outside interference or access via the Internet.

Folder

A structure for containing electronic files. In some operating systems, it is called a directory.

Fonts

Sets of typefaces (or characters) that come in different styles and sizes.

Freeware

Software created by people who are willing to give it away for the satisfaction of sharing or knowing they helped to simplify other people's lives. It may be free-standing software, or it may add functionality to existing software.

FTP

File Transfer Protocol, a format and set of rules for transferring files from a host to a remote computer.

Gigabyte (GB)

1024 megabytes. Also called gig.

Glitch

The cause of an unexpected malfunction.

Gopher

An Internet search tool that allows users to access textual information through a series of menus, or if using FTP, through downloads.

GUI

Graphical User Interface, a system that simplifies selecting computer commands by enabling the user to point to symbols or illustrations (called icons) on the computer screen with a mouse.

Groupware

Software that allows networked individuals to form groups and collaborate on documents, programs, or databases.

Hacker

A person with technical expertise who experiments with computer systems to determine how to develop additional features. Hackers are occasionally requested by system administrators to try and break into systems via a network to test security. The term hacker is sometimes incorrectly used interchangeably with cracker. A hacker is called a white hat and a cracker a black hat.

Hard copy

A paper printout of what you have prepared on the computer.

Hard drive

Another name for the hard disc that stores information in a computer.

Hardware

The physical and mechanical components of a computer system, such as the electronic circuitry, chips, monitor, disks, disk drives, keyboard, modem, and printer.

Home page

The main page of a Web site used to greet visitors, provide information about the site, or to direct the viewer to other pages on the site.

HTML

Hypertext Markup Language, a standard of text markup conventions used for documents on the World Wide Web. Browsers interpret the codes to give the text structure and formatting (such as bold, blue, or italic).

HTTP

Hypertext Transfer Protocol, a common system used to request and send HTML documents on the World Wide Web. It is the first portion of all URL addresses on the World Wide Web.

HTTPS

Hypertext Transfer Protocol Secure, often used in intracompany internet sites. Passwords are required to gain access.

Hyperlink

Text or an image that is connected by hypertext coding to a different location. By selecting the text or image with a mouse, the computer jumps to (or displays) the linked text.

Hypermedia

Integrates audio, graphics, and/or video through links embedded in the main program.

Hypertext

A system for organizing text through links, as opposed to a menu-driven hierarchy such as Gopher. Most Web pages include hypertext links to other pages at that site, or to other sites on the World Wide Web.

Icons

Symbols or illustrations appearing on the computer screen that indicate program files or other computer functions.

Input

Data that goes into a computer device.

Input device

A device, such as a keyboard, stylus and tablet, mouse, puck, or microphone, that allows input of information (letters, numbers, sound, video) to a computer.

Instant messaging (IM)

A chat application that allows two or more people to communicate over the Internet via real-time keyed-in messages.

Interface

The interconnections that allow a device, a program, or a person to interact. Hardware interfaces are the cables that connect the device to its power source and to other devices. Software interfaces allow the program to communicate with other programs (such as the operating system), and user interfaces allow the user to communicate with the program (e.g., via mouse, menu commands, icons, voice commands, etc.).

Internet

An international conglomeration of interconnected computer networks. Begun in the late 1960s, it was developed in the 1970s to allow government and university researchers to share information. The Internet is not controlled by any single group or organization. Its original focus was research and communications, but it continues to expand, offering a wide array of resources for business and home users.

IP (Internet Protocol) address

An Internet Protocol address is a unique set of numbers used to locate another computer on a network. The format of an IP address is a 32-bit string of four numbers separated by periods. Each number can be from 0 to 255 (i.e., 1.154.10.255). Within a closed network IP addresses may be assigned at random, however, IP addresses of web servers must be registered to avoid duplicates.

Java

An object-oriented programming language designed specifically for programs (particularly multimedia) to be used over the Internet. Java allows programmers to create small programs or applications (applets) to enhance Web sites.

JavaScript/ECMA script

A programming language used almost exclusively to manipulate content on a web page. Common JavaScript functions include validating forms on a web page, creating dynamic page navigation menus, and image rollovers.

Kilobyte (K or KB)

Equal to 1,024 bytes.

Linux

A UNIX - like, open-source operating system developed primarily by Linus Torvalds. Linux is free and runs on many platforms, including both PCs and Macintoshes. Linux is an open-source operating system, meaning that the source code of the operating system is freely available to the public. Programmers may redistribute and modify the code, as long as they don't collect royalties on their work or deny access to their code. Since development is not restricted to a single corporation more programmers can debug and improve the source code faster.

Laptop and notebook

Small, lightweight, portable battery-powered computers that can fit onto your lap. They each have a thin, flat, liquid crystal display screen.

Macro

A script that operates a series of commands to perform a function. It is set up to automate repetitive tasks.

Mac OS

An operating system with a graphical user interface, developed by Apple for Macintosh computers. Current System X.1.(10) combines the traditional Mac interface with a strong underlying UNIX. Operating system for increased performance and stability.

Megabyte (MB)

Equal to 1,048,576 bytes, usually rounded off to one million bytes (also called a meg).

Memory

Temporary storage for information, including applications and documents. The information must be stored to a permanent device, such as a hard disc or CD-ROM before the power is turned off, or the information will be lost. Computer memory is measured in terms of the amount of information it can store, commonly in megabytes or gigabytes.

Menu

A context-related list of options that users can choose from.

Menu bar

The horizontal strip across the top of an application's window. Each word on the strip has a context sensitive drop-down menu containing features and actions that are available for the application in use.

Merge

To combine two or more files into a single file.

MHz

An abbreviation for **Megahertz, or one million hertz.** One MHz represents one million clock cycles per second and is the measure of a computer microprocessor's speed. For example, a microprocessor that runs at 300 MHz executes 300 million cycles per second. Each instruction a computer receives takes a fixed number of clock cycles to carry out, therefore the more cycles a computer can execute per second, the faster its programs run. Megahertz is also a unit of measure for bandwidth.

Microprocessor

A complete central processing unit (CPU) contained on a single silicon chip.

Minimize

A term used in a GUI operating system that uses windows. It refers to reducing a window to an icon, or a label at the bottom of the screen, allowing another window to be viewed.

Modem

A device that connects two computers together over a telephone or cable line by converting the computer's data into an audio signal. Modem is a contraction for the process it performs : modulate-demodulate.

Monitor

A video display terminal.

Mouse

A small hand-held device, similar to a trackball, used to control the position of the cursor on the video display; movements of the mouse on a desktop correspond to movements of the cursor on the screen.

MP3

Compact audio and video file format. The small size of the files makes them easy to download and e-mail. Format used in portable playback devices.

Multimedia

Software programs that combine text and graphics with sound, video, and animation. A multimedia PC contains the hardware to support these capabilities.

MS-DOS

An early operating system developed by Microsoft Corporation (Microsoft Disc Operating System).

Network

A system of interconnected computers.

Open source

Computer programs whose original source code was revealed to the general public so that it could be developed openly. Software licensed as open source can be freely changed or adapted to new uses, meaning that the source code of the operating system is freely available to the public. Programmers may redistribute and modify the code, as long as they don't collect royalties on their work or deny access to their code. Since development is not restricted to a single corporation more programmers can debug and improve the source code faster.

Operating system

A set of instructions that tell a computer on how to operate when it is turned on. It sets up a filing system to store files and tells the computer how to display information on a video display. Most PC operating systems are DOS (disc operated system) systems, meaning the instructions are stored on a disc (as opposed to being originally stored in the microprocessors of the computer). Other well-known operating systems include UNIX, Linux, Macintosh, and Windows.

Output

Data that come out of a computer device. For example, information displayed on the monitor, sound from the speakers, and information printed to paper.

Palm

A hand-held computer.

PC

Personal computer. Generally refers to computers running Windows with a Pentium processor.

PC board

Printed Circuit board, a board printed or etched with a circuit and processors. Power supplies, information storage devices, or changers are attached.

PDA

Personal Digital Assistant, a hand-held computer that can store daily appointments, phone numbers, addresses, and other important information. Most PDAs link to a desktop or laptop computer to download or upload information.

PDF

Portable Document Format, a format presented by Adobe Acrobat that allows documents to be shared over a variety of operating systems. Documents can contain words and pictures and be formatted to have electronic links to other parts of the document or to places on the web.

Pentium chip

Intel's fifth generation of sophisticated high-speed microprocessors. Pentium means the fifth element.

Peripheral

Any external device attached to a computer to

enhance operation. Examples include external hard drive, scanner, printer, speakers, keyboard, mouse, trackball, stylus and tablet, and joystick.

Personal computer (PC)

A single-user computer containing a central processing unit (CPU) and one or more memory circuits.

Petabyte

A measure of memory or storage capacity and is approximately a thousand terabytes.

Petaflop

A theoretical measure of a computer's speed and can be expressed as a thousand-trillion floating-point operations per second.

Platform

The operating system, such as UNIX, Macintosh, Windows, on which a computer is based.

Plug and play

Computer hardware or peripherals that come set up with necessary software so that when attached to a computer, they are recognized by the computer and are ready to use.

Pop-up menu

A menu window that opens vertically or horizontally on-screen to display context-related options. Also called drop-down menu or pull-down menu.

Power PC

A competitor of the Pentium chip. It is a new generation of powerful sophisticated microprocessors produced from an Apple-IBM-Motorola alliance.

Printer

A mechanical device for printing a computer's output on paper. There are three major types of printer:

> **Dot matrix** - creates individual letters, made up of a series of tiny ink dots, by punching a ribbon with the ends of tiny wires. (This type of printer is most often used in industrial settings, such as direct mail for labelling.)
>
> **Ink jet** - sprays tiny droplets of ink particles onto paper.
>
> **Laser** - uses a beam of light to reproduce the image of each page using a magnetic charge that attracts dry toner that is transferred to paper and sealed with heat.

Program

A precise series of instructions written in a computer language that tells the computer what to do and how to do it. Programs are also called software or applications.

Programming language

A series of instructions written by a programmer according to a given set of rules or conventions (syntax). High-level programming languages are independent of the device on which the application (or program) will eventually run; low-level languages are specific to each program or platform. Programming language instructions are converted into programs in language specific to a particular machine or operating system (machine language). So that the computer can interpret and carry out the instructions. Some common programming languages are BASIC, C, C++, dBASE, FORTRAN, and Perl.

Puck

An input device, like a mouse. It has a magnifying glass with crosshairs on the front of it that allows the operator to position it precisely when tracing a drawing for use with CAD-CAM software.

Pull-down menu

A menu window that opens vertically on-screen to

display context-related options. Also called drop-down menu or pop-up menu.

Push technology

Internet tool that delivers specific information directly to a user's desktop, eliminating the need to surf for it. PointCast, which delivers news in user-defined categories, is a popular example of this technology.

QuickTime

Audio-visual software that allows movie-delivery via the Internet and e-mail. QuickTime images are viewed on a monitor.

RAID

Redundant Array of Inexpensive Disks, a method of spreading information across several disks set up to act as a unit, using two different techniques:

- **Disk striping** - storing a bit of information across several discs (instead of storing it all on one disc and hoping that the disc doesn't crash).

- **Disk mirroring** - simultaneously storing a copy of information on another disc so that the information can be recovered if the main disc crashes.

RAM

Random Access Memory, one of two basic types of memory. Portions of programs are stored in RAM when the program is launched so that the program will run faster. Though a PC has a fixed amount of RAM, only portions of it will be accessed by the computer at any given time. Also called memory.

Right-click

Using the right mouse button to open context-sensitive drop-down menus.

ROM

Read-Only Memory, one of two basic types of memory. ROM contains only permanent information put there by the manufacturer. Information in ROM cannot be altered, nor can the memory be dynamically allocated by the computer or its operator.

Scanner

An electronic device that uses light-sensing equipment to scan paper images such as text, photos, and illustrations and translate the images into signals that the computer can then store, modify, or distribute.

Search engine

Software that makes it possible to look for and retrieve material on the Internet, particularly the Web. Some popular search engines are Alta Vista, Google, HotBot, Yahoo!, Web Crawler, and Lycos.

Server

A computer that shares its resources and information with other computers, called clients, on a network.

Shareware

Software created by people who are willing to sell it at low cost or no cost for the gratification of sharing. It may be freestanding software, or it may add functionality to existing software.

Software

Computer programs; also called applications.

Spider

A process search engines use to investigate new pages on a web site and collect the information that needs to be put in their indices.

Spreadsheet

Software that allows one to calculate numbers in a

format that is similar to pages in a conventional ledger.

Storage

Devices used to store massive amounts of information so that it can be readily retrieved. Devices include RAIDs, CD-ROMs, DVDs.

Streaming

Taking packets of information (sound or visual) from the Internet and storing it in temporary files to allow it to play in continuous flow.

Stylus and tablet

An input device similar to a mouse. The stylus is pen shaped. It is used to draw on a tablet (like drawing on paper) and the tablet transfers the information to the computer. The tablet responds to pressure. The firmer the pressure used to draw, the thicker the line appears.

Surfing

Exploring the Internet.

Surge protector

A controller to protect the computer and make up for variances in voltage.

Telnet

A way to communicate with a remote computer over a network.

Trackball

Input device that controls the position of the cursor on the screen; the unit is mounted near the keyboard, and movement is controlled by moving a ball.

Terabytes (TB)

A thousand gigabytes.

Teraflop

A measure of a computer's speed. It can be expressed as a trillion floating-point operations per second.

Trojan Horse

See Virus

UNIX

A very powerful operating system used as the basis of many high-end computer applications.

Upload

The process of transferring information from a

computer to a web site (or other remote location on a network). To transfer information from a computer to a web site (or other remote location on a network).

URL

Uniform Resource Locator.

The protocol for identifying a document on the Web.

A Web address (e.g., www.tutorialspoint.com). A URL is unique to each user. See also domain.

UPS

Universal Power Supply or Uninterruptible Power Supply. An electrical power supply that includes a battery to provide enough power to a computer during an outage to back-up data and properly shut down.

USB

A multiple-socket USB connector that allows several USB-compatible devices to be connected to a computer.

USENET

A large unmoderated and unedited bulletin board on the Internet that offers thousands of forums, called newsgroups. These range from newsgroups exchanging information on scientific advances to celebrity fan clubs.

User friendly

A program or device whose use is intuitive to people with a non-technical background.

Video teleconferencing

A remote "face-to-face chat," when two or more people using a webcam and an Internet telephone connection chat online. The webcam enables both live voice and video.

Virtual reality (VR)

A technology that allows one to experience and interact with images in a simulated three-dimensional environment. For example, you could design a room in a house on your computer and actually feel that you are walking around in it even though it was never built. (The Holodeck in the science-fiction TV series Star Trek : Voyager would be the ultimate virtual reality.) Current technology requires the user to wear a special helmet, viewing goggles, gloves, and other equipment that transmits and receives information from the computer.

Virus

An unauthorized piece of computer code attached to

a computer program or portions of a computer system that secretly copies itself from one computer to another by shared discs and over telephone and cable lines. It can destroy information stored on the computer, and in extreme cases, can destroy operability. Computers can be protected from viruses if the operator utilizes good virus prevention software and keeps the virus definitions up to date. Most viruses are not programmed to spread themselves. They have to be sent to another computer by e-mail, sharing, or applications. The worm is an exception, because it is programmed to replicate itself by sending copies to other computers listed in the e-mail address book in the computer. There are many kinds of viruses, for example:

> Boot viruses place some of their code in the start-up disk sector to automatically execute when booting. Therefore, when an infected machine boots, the virus loads and runs.

> File viruses attached to program files (files with the extension .exe). When you run the infected program, the virus code executes.

> Macro viruses copy their macros to templates and/or other application document files.

> Trojan Horse is a malicious, security-breaking program that is disguised as something being such as a screen saver or game.

Worm launches an application that destroys information on your hard drive. It also sends a copy of the virus to everyone in the computer's e-mail address book.

WAV

A sound format (pronounced wave) used to reproduce sounds on a computer.

Webcam

A video camera/computer setup that takes live images and sends them to a Web browser.

Window

A portion of a computer display used in a graphical interface that enables users to select commands by pointing to illustrations or symbols with a mouse. "Windows" is also the name Microsoft adopted for its popular operating system.

World Wide Web ("WWW" or "the Web")

A network of servers on the Internet that use hypertext-linked databases and files. It was developed in 1989 by Tim Berners-Lee, a British computer scientist, and is now the primary platform of the Internet. The feature that distinguishes the Web from other Internet applications is its ability to display graphics in addition to text.

Word processor

A computer system or program for setting, editing, revising, correcting, storing, and printing text.

WYSIWYG

What You See Is What You Get. When using most word processors, page layout programs (See desktop publishing), and web page design programs, words and images will be displayed on the monitor as they will look on the printed page or web page.

Telnet

A way to communicate with a remote computer over a network.

Trackball

Input device that controls the position of the cursor on the screen; the unit is mounted near the keyboard, and movement is controlled by moving a ball.

Terabytes (TB)

A thousand gigabytes.

Teraflop

A measure of a computer's speed. It can be expressed as a trillion floating-point operations per second.

Trojan Horse

See virus.

UNIX

A very powerful operating system used as the basis of many high-end computer applications.

Upload

The process of transferring information from a computer to a web site (or other remote location on a network). To transfer information from a computer to a web site (or other remote location on a network).

URL

Uniform Resource Locator.

The protocol for identifying a document on the Web.

A Web address (e.g., www.tutorialspoint.com). A URL is unique to each user. See also domain.

UPS

Universal Power Supply or Uninterruptible Power Supply. An electrical power supply that includes a battery to provide enough power to a computer during an outage to back-up data and properly shut down.

USB

A multiple-socket USB connector that allows several USB-compatible devices to be connected to a computer.

USENET

A large unmoderated and unedited bulletin board on the Internet that offers thousands of forums, called newsgroups. These range from newsgroups exchanging information on scientific advances to celebrity fan clubs.

User friendly

A program or device whose use is intuitive to people with a non-technical background.

Video teleconferencing

A remote "face-to-face chat," when two or more people using a webcam and an Internet telephone connection chat online. The webcam enables both live voice and video.

Virtual reality (VR)

A technology that allows one to experience and interact with images in a simulated three-dimensional environment. For example, you could design a room in a house on your computer and actually feel that you are walking around in it even though it was never built. (The Holodeck in the science-fiction TV series Star Trek : Voyager would be the ultimate virtual reality.) Current technology requires the user to wear a special helmet, viewing goggles, gloves, and other equipment that transmits and receives information from the computer.

Virus

An unauthorized piece of computer code attached to a computer program or portions of a computer system that secretly copies itself from one computer to another by shared discs and over telephone and cable lines. It can destroy information stored on the computer, and in extreme cases, can destroy operability. Computers can be protected from viruses if the operator utilizes good virus prevention software and keeps the virus definitions up to date. Most viruses are not programmed to spread themselves. They have to be sent to another computer by e-mail, sharing, or applications. The worm is an exception, because it is programmed to replicate itself by sending copies to other computers listed in the e-mail address book in the computer. There are many kinds of viruses, for example:

> Boot viruses place some of their code in the start-up disk sector to automatically execute when booting. Therefore, when an infected machine boots, the virus loads and runs.

> File viruses attached to program files (files with the extension .exe). When you run the infected program, the virus code executes.

> Macro viruses copy their macros to templates and/or other application document files.

> Trojan Horse is a malicious, security-breaking program that is disguised as something being such as a screen saver or game.

> Worm launches an application that destroys information on your hard drive. It also sends a copy of the virus to everyone in the computer's e-mail address book.

WAV

A sound format (pronounced wave) used to reproduce sounds on a computer.

Webcam

A video camera/computer setup that takes live images and sends them to a Web browser.

Window

A portion of a computer display used in a graphical interface that enables users to select commands by pointing to illustrations or symbols with a mouse. "Windows" is also the name Microsoft adopted for its popular operating system.

World Wide Web ("WWW" or "the Web")

A network of servers on the Internet that use hypertext-linked databases and files. It was developed in 1989 by Tim Berners-Lee, a British computer scientist, and is now the primary platform of the Internet. The feature that distinguishes the Web from other Internet applications is its ability to display graphics in addition to text.

Word processor

A computer system or program for setting, editing, revising, correcting, storing, and printing text.

WYSIWYG

What You See Is What You Get. When using most word processors, page layout programs (See desktop publishing), and web page design programs, words and images will be displayed on the monitor as they will look on the printed page or web page.

Applet

A small Java application that is downloaded by an ActiveX or Java-enabled web browser. Once it has been downloaded, the applet will run on the user's computer. Common applets include financial calculators and web drawing programs.

Application

Computer software that performs a task or set of tasks, such as word processing or drawing. Applications are also referred to as programs.

ASCII

American Standard Code for Information Interchange, an encoding system for converting keyboard characters and instructions into the binary number code that the computer understands.

Bandwidth

The capacity of a networked connection. Bandwidth determines how much data can be sent along the networked wires. Bandwidth is particularly important for Internet connections, since greater bandwidth also means faster downloads.

Binary code

The most basic language a computer understands, it is composed of a series of 0s and 1s. The computer interprets the code to form numbers, letters, punctuation marks, and symbols.

Bit

The smallest piece of computer information, either the number 0 or 1. In short they are called binary digits.

Boot

To start up a computer. Cold boot means restarting computer after the power is turned off. Warm boot means restarting computer without turning off the power.

Browser

Software used to navigate the Internet. Google Chrome, Firefox, Netscape Navigator and Microsoft Internet Explorer are today's most popular browsers for accessing the World Wide Web.

Bug

A malfunction due to an error in the program or a defect in the equipment.

Byte

Most computers use combinations of eight bits, called bytes, to represent one character of data or instructions. For example, the word **cat** has three characters, and it would be represented by three bytes.

Cache

A small data-memory storage area that a computer can use to instantly re-access data instead of re-reading the data from the original source, such as a hard drive. Browsers use a cache to store web pages so that the user may view them again without reconnecting to the Web.

CAD-CAM

Computer Aided Drawing - Computer Aided Manufacturing. The instructions stored in a computer that will be translated to very precise operating instructions to a robot, such as for assembling cars or laser-cutting signage.

CD-ROM

Compact Disc Read-Only Memory, an optically read disc designed to hold information such as music, reference materials, or computer software. A single CD-ROM can hold around 640 megabytes of data, enough for several encyclopaedias. Most software programs are now delivered on CD-ROMs.

CGI

Common Gateway Interface, a programming standard that allows visitors to fill out form fields on a Web page and have that information interact with a database, possibly coming back to the user as another Web page. CGI may also refer to Computer-Generated Imaging, the process in which sophisticated computer programs create still and animated graphics, such as special effects for movies.

Chat

Typing text into a message box on a screen to engage in dialogue with one or more people via the Internet or other network.

Chip

A tiny wafer of silicon containing miniature electric circuits that can store millions of bits of information.

Client

A single user of a network application that is operated from a server. A client/server architecture allows many people to use the same data simultaneously. The program's main component (the data) resides on a centralized server, with smaller components (user interface) on each client.

Cookie

A text file sent by a Web server that is stored on the hard drive of a computer and relays back to the Web server things about the user, his or her computer, and/or his or her computer activities.

CPU

Central Processing Unit. The brain of the computer.

Cracker

A person who breaks in to a computer through a network, without authorization and with mischievous or destructive intent.

Crash

A hardware or software problem that causes information to be lost or the computer to malfunction. Sometimes a crash can cause permanent damage to a computer.

Cursor

A moving position-indicator displayed on a computer monitor that shows a computer operator where the next action or operation will take place.

Cyberspace

Slang for internet ie. An international conglomeration of interconnected computer networks. Begun in the late 1960s, it was developed in the 1970s to allow government and university researchers to share information. The Internet is not controlled by any single group or organization. Its original focus was research and communications, but it continues to expand, offering a wide array of resources for business and home users.

Database

A collection of similar information stored in a file, such as a database of addresses. This information may be created and stored in a database management system (DBMS).

Debug

Slang. To find and correct equipment defects or program malfunctions.

Default

The pre-defined configuration of a system or an application. In most programs, the defaults can be changed to reflect personal preferences.

Desktop

The main directory of the user interface. Desktops usually contain icons that represent links to the hard drive, a network (if there is one), and a trash or recycling can for files to be deleted. It can also display icons of frequently used applications, as requested by the user.

Desktop publishing

The production of publication-quality documents using a personal computer in combination with text, graphics, and page layout programs.

Directory

A repository where all files are kept on computer.

Disk

Two distinct types. The names refer to the media inside the container:

A hard disc stores vast amounts of data. It is usually inside the computer but can be a separate peripheral on the outside. Hard discs are made up of several rigid coated metal discs. Currently, hard discs can store 15 to 30 Gb (gigabytes).

A floppy disc, 3.5" square, usually inserted into the computer and can store about 1.4 megabytes of data. The 3.5" square floppies have a very thin, flexible disc inside. There is also an intermediate-sized floppy disc, trademarked Zip discs, which can store 250 megabytes of data.

Disk drive

The equipment that operates a hard or floppy disc.

Domain

Represents an IP (Internet Protocol) address or set of IP addresses that comprise a domain. The domain name appears in URLs to identify web pages or in email addresses. For example, the email address for the First Lady is first.lady@whitehouse.gov, whitehouse.gov, being the domain name. Each domain name ends with a suffix that indicates what top level domain it belongs to. These are : .com for commercial, .gov for government, .org for organization, .edu for educational institution, .biz for business, .info for information, .tv for television, .ws for website. Domain suffixes may also indicate the country in which the domain is registered. No two parties can ever hold the same domain name.

Domain name

The name of a network or computer linked to the Internet. Domains are defined by a common IP address or set of similar IP (Internet Protocol) addresses.

Download

The process of transferring information from a web site (or other remote location on a network) to the computer. It is possible to download a file which include text, image, audio, video and many others.

DOS

Disk Operating System. An operating system designed for early IBM-compatible PCs.

Drop-down menu

A menu window that opens vertically on-screen to display context-related options. Also called pop-up menu or pull-down menu.

DSL

Digital Subscriber Line, a method of connecting to the Internet via a phone line. A DSL connection uses copper telephone lines but is able to relay data at much higher speeds than modems and does not interfere with telephone use.

DVD

Digital Video Disc. Similar to a CD-ROM, it stores and plays both audio and video.

E-book

An electronic (usually hand-held) reading device that allows a person to view digitally stored reading materials.

Email

Electronic mail; messages, including memos or letters, sent electronically between networked computers that may be across the office or around the world.

Emoticon

A text-based expression of emotion created from ASCII characters that mimics a facial expression when viewed with your head tilted to the left. Here are some examples:

> Smiling
> Frowning
> Winking
>
> Crying

Encryption

The process of transmitting scrambled data so that only authorized recipients can unscramble it. For instance, encryption is used to scramble credit card information when purchases are made over the Internet.

Ethernet

A type of network.

Ethernet card

A board inside a computer to which a network cable can be attached.

File

A set of data that is stored in the computer.

Firewall

A set of security programs that protect a computer from outside interference or access via the Internet.

Folder

A structure for containing electronic files. In some operating systems, it is called a directory.

Fonts

Sets of typefaces (or characters) that come in

different styles and sizes.

Freeware

Software created by people who are willing to give it away for the satisfaction of sharing or knowing they helped to simplify other people's lives. It may be free-standing software, or it may add functionality to existing software.

FTP

File Transfer Protocol, a format and set of rules for transferring files from a host to a remote computer.

Gigabyte (GB)

1024 megabytes. Also called gig.

Glitch

The cause of an unexpected malfunction.

Gopher

An Internet search tool that allows users to access textual information through a series of menus, or if using FTP, through downloads.

GUI

Graphical User Interface, a system that simplifies

selecting computer commands by enabling the user to point to symbols or illustrations (called icons) on the computer screen with a mouse.

Groupware

Software that allows networked individuals to form groups and collaborate on documents, programs, or databases.

Hacker

A person with technical expertise who experiments with computer systems to determine how to develop additional features. Hackers are occasionally requested by system administrators to try and break into systems via a network to test security. The term hacker is sometimes incorrectly used interchangeably with cracker. A hacker is called a white hat and a cracker a black hat.

Hard copy

A paper printout of what you have prepared on the computer.

Hard drive

Another name for the hard disc that stores information in a computer.

Hardware

The physical and mechanical components of a computer system, such as the electronic circuitry, chips, monitor, disks, disk drives, keyboard, modem, and printer.

Home page

The main page of a Web site used to greet visitors, provide information about the site, or to direct the viewer to other pages on the site.

HTML

Hypertext Markup Language, a standard of text markup conventions used for documents on the World Wide Web. Browsers interpret the codes to give the text structure and formatting (such as bold, blue, or italic).

HTTP

Hypertext Transfer Protocol, a common system used to request and send HTML documents on the World Wide Web. It is the first portion of all URL addresses on the World Wide Web.

HTTPS

Hypertext Transfer Protocol Secure, often used in intracompany internet sites. Passwords are required to gain access.

Hyperlink

Text or an image that is connected by hypertext coding to a different location. By selecting the text or image with a mouse, the computer jumps to (or displays) the linked text.

Hypermedia

Integrates audio, graphics, and/or video through links embedded in the main program.

Hypertext

A system for organizing text through links, as opposed to a menu-driven hierarchy such as Gopher. Most Web pages include hypertext links to other pages at that site, or to other sites on the World Wide Web.

Icons

Symbols or illustrations appearing on the computer screen that indicate program files or other computer functions.

Input

Data that goes into a computer device.

Input device

A device, such as a keyboard, stylus and tablet, mouse, puck, or microphone, that allows input of information (letters, numbers, sound, video) to a computer.

Instant messaging (IM)

A chat application that allows two or more people to communicate over the Internet via real-time keyed-in messages.

Interface

The interconnections that allow a device, a program, or a person to interact. Hardware interfaces are the cables that connect the device to its power source and to other devices. Software interfaces allow the program to communicate with other programs (such as the operating system), and user interfaces allow the user to communicate with the program (e.g., via mouse, menu commands, icons, voice commands, etc.).

Internet

An international conglomeration of interconnected computer networks. Begun in the late 1960s, it was developed in the 1970s to allow government and university researchers to share information. The Internet is not controlled by any single group or organization. Its original focus was research and communications, but it continues to expand, offering a wide array of resources for business and home users.

IP (Internet Protocol) address

An Internet Protocol address is a unique set of numbers used to locate another computer on a network. The format of an IP address is a 32-bit string of four numbers separated by periods. Each number can be from 0 to 255 (i.e., 1.154.10.255). Within a closed network IP addresses may be assigned at random, however, IP addresses of web servers must be registered to avoid duplicates.

Java

An object-oriented programming language designed specifically for programs (particularly multimedia) to be used over the Internet. Java allows programmers to create small programs or applications (applets) to enhance Web sites.

JavaScript/ECMA script

A programming language used almost exclusively to manipulate content on a web page. Common JavaScript functions include validating forms on a web page, creating dynamic page navigation menus, and image rollovers.

Kilobyte (K or KB)

Equal to 1,024 bytes.

Linux

A UNIX - like, open-source operating system developed primarily by Linus Torvalds. Linux is free and runs on many platforms, including both PCs and Macintoshes. Linux is an open-source operating system, meaning that the source code of the operating system is freely available to the public. Programmers may redistribute and modify the code, as long as they don't collect royalties on their work or deny access to their code. Since development is not restricted to a single corporation more programmers can debug and improve the source code faster.

Laptop and notebook

Small, lightweight, portable battery-powered computers that can fit onto your lap. They each have a thin, flat, liquid crystal display screen.

Macro

A script that operates a series of commands to perform a function. It is set up to automate repetitive tasks.

Mac OS

An operating system with a graphical user interface, developed by Apple for Macintosh computers. Current System X.1.(10) combines the traditional Mac interface with a strong underlying UNIX. Operating system for increased performance and stability.

Megabyte (MB)

Equal to 1,048,576 bytes, usually rounded off to one million bytes (also called a meg).

Memory

Temporary storage for information, including applications and documents. The information must be stored to a permanent device, such as a hard disc or CD-ROM before the power is turned off, or the information will be lost. Computer memory is measured in terms of the amount of information it can store, commonly in megabytes or gigabytes.

Menu

A context-related list of options that users can choose from.

Menu bar

The horizontal strip across the top of an

application's window. Each word on the strip has a context sensitive drop-down menu containing features and actions that are available for the application in use.

Merge

To combine two or more files into a single file.

MHz

An abbreviation for **Megahertz,** or **one million hertz.** One MHz represents one million clock cycles per second and is the measure of a computer microprocessor's speed. For example, a microprocessor that runs at 300 MHz executes 300 million cycles per second. Each instruction a computer receives takes a fixed number of clock cycles to carry out, therefore the more cycles a computer can execute per second, the faster its programs run. Megahertz is also a unit of measure for bandwidth.

Microprocessor

A complete central processing unit (CPU) contained on a single silicon chip.

Minimize

A term used in a GUI operating system that uses windows. It refers to reducing a window to an icon, or a label at the bottom of the screen, allowing another window to be viewed.

Modem

A device that connects two computers together over a telephone or cable line by converting the computer's data into an audio signal. Modem is a contraction for the process it performs : modulate-demodulate.

Monitor

A video display terminal.

Mouse

A small hand-held device, similar to a trackball, used to control the position of the cursor on the video display; movements of the mouse on a desktop correspond to movements of the cursor on the screen.

MP3

Compact audio and video file format. The small size of the files makes them easy to download and e-mail. Format used in portable playback devices.

Multimedia

Software programs that combine text and graphics with sound, video, and animation. A multimedia PC contains the hardware to support these capabilities.

MS-DOS

An early operating system developed by Microsoft Corporation (Microsoft Disc Operating System).

Network

A system of interconnected computers.

Open source

Computer programs whose original source code was revealed to the general public so that it could be developed openly. Software licensed as open source can be freely changed or adapted to new uses, meaning that the source code of the operating system is freely available to the public. Programmers may redistribute and modify the code, as long as they don't collect royalties on their work or deny access to their code. Since development is not restricted to a single corporation more programmers can debug and improve the source code faster.

Operating system

A set of instructions that tell a computer on how to operate when it is turned on. It sets up a filing system to store files and tells the computer how to display information on a video display. Most PC operating systems are DOS (disc operated system) systems, meaning the instructions are stored on a disc (as opposed to being originally stored in the microprocessors of the computer). Other well-known operating systems include UNIX, Linux, Macintosh, and Windows.

Output

Data that come out of a computer device. For example, information displayed on the monitor, sound from the speakers, and information printed to paper.

Palm

A hand-held computer.

PC

Personal computer. Generally refers to computers running Windows with a Pentium processor.

PC board

Printed Circuit board, a board printed or etched with a circuit and processors. Power supplies, information storage devices, or changers are attached.

PDA

Personal Digital Assistant, a hand-held computer that can store daily appointments, phone numbers, addresses, and other important information. Most PDAs link to a desktop or laptop computer to download or upload information.

PDF

Portable Document Format, a format presented by Adobe Acrobat that allows documents to be shared over a variety of operating systems. Documents can contain words and pictures and be formatted to have electronic links to other parts of the document or to places on the web.

Pentium chip

Intel's fifth generation of sophisticated high-speed microprocessors. Pentium means the fifth element.

Peripheral

Any external device attached to a computer to enhance operation. Examples include external hard drive, scanner, printer, speakers, keyboard, mouse, trackball, stylus and tablet, and joystick.

Personal computer (PC)

A single-user computer containing a central processing unit (CPU) and one or more memory circuits.

Petabyte

A measure of memory or storage capacity and is approximately a thousand terabytes.

Petaflop

A theoretical measure of a computer's speed and can be expressed as a thousand-trillion floating-point operations per second.

Platform

The operating system, such as UNIX, Macintosh, Windows, on which a computer is based.

Plug and play

Computer hardware or peripherals that come set up with necessary software so that when attached to a computer, they are recognized by the computer and are ready to use.

Pop-up menu

A menu window that opens vertically or horizontally on-screen to display context-related options. Also called drop-down menu or pull-down menu.

Power PC

A competitor of the Pentium chip. It is a new generation of powerful sophisticated microprocessors produced from an Apple-IBM-Motorola alliance.

Printer

A mechanical device for printing a computer's output on paper. There are three major types of printer:

> **Dot matrix** - creates individual letters, made up of a series of tiny ink dots, by punching a ribbon with the ends of tiny wires. (This type of printer is most often used in industrial settings, such as direct mail for labelling.)
>
> **Ink jet** - sprays tiny droplets of ink particles onto paper.
>
> **Laser** - uses a beam of light to reproduce the image of each page using a magnetic charge that attracts dry toner that is transferred to paper and sealed with heat.

Program

A precise series of instructions written in a computer language that tells the computer what to do and how to do it. Programs are also called software or applications.

Programming language

A series of instructions written by a programmer according to a given set of rules or conventions (syntax). High-level programming languages are independent of the device on which the application (or program) will eventually run; low-level languages are specific to each program or platform. Programming language instructions are converted into programs in language specific to a particular machine or operating system (machine language). So that the computer can interpret and carry out the instructions. Some common programming languages are BASIC, C, C++, dBASE, FORTRAN, and Perl.

Puck

An input device, like a mouse. It has a magnifying glass with crosshairs on the front of it that allows the operator to position it precisely when tracing a drawing for use with CAD-CAM software.

Pull-down menu

A menu window that opens vertically on-screen to display context-related options. Also called drop-down menu or pop-up menu.

Push technology

Internet tool that delivers specific information directly to a user's desktop, eliminating the need to surf for it. PointCast, which delivers news in user-defined categories, is a popular example of this technology.

QuickTime

Audio-visual software that allows movie-delivery via the Internet and e-mail. QuickTime images are viewed on a monitor.

RAID

Redundant Array of Inexpensive Disks, a method of spreading information across several disks set up to act as a unit, using two different techniques:

- **Disk striping -** storing a bit of information across several discs (instead of storing it all on one disc and hoping that the disc doesn't crash).

- **Disk mirroring -** simultaneously storing a copy of information on another disc so that the information can be recovered if the main disc crashes.

RAM

Random Access Memory, one of two basic types of memory. Portions of programs are stored in RAM when the program is launched so that the program will run faster. Though a PC has a fixed amount of RAM, only portions of it will be accessed by the computer at any given time. Also called memory.

Right-click

Using the right mouse button to open context-sensitive drop-down menus.

ROM

Read-Only Memory, one of two basic types of memory. ROM contains only permanent information put there by the manufacturer. Information in ROM cannot be altered, nor can the memory be dynamically allocated by the computer or its operator.

Scanner

An electronic device that uses light-sensing equipment to scan paper images such as text, photos, and illustrations and translate the images into signals that the computer can then store, modify, or distribute.

Search engine

Software that makes it possible to look for and retrieve material on the Internet, particularly the Web. Some popular search engines are Alta Vista, Google, HotBot, Yahoo!, Web Crawler, and Lycos.

Server

A computer that shares its resources and

information with other computers, called clients, on a network.

Shareware

Software created by people who are willing to sell it at low cost or no cost for the gratification of sharing. It may be freestanding software, or it may add functionality to existing software.

Software

Computer programs; also called applications.

Spider

A process search engines use to investigate new pages on a web site and collect the information that needs to be put in their indices.

Spreadsheet

Software that allows one to calculate numbers in a format that is similar to pages in a conventional ledger.

Storage

Devices used to store massive amounts of information so that it can be readily retrieved. Devices include RAIDs, CD-ROMs, DVDs.

Streaming

Taking packets of information (sound or visual) from the Internet and storing it in temporary files to allow it to play in continuous flow.

Stylus and tablet

An input device similar to a mouse. The stylus is pen shaped. It is used to draw on a tablet (like drawing on paper) and the tablet transfers the information to the computer. The tablet responds to pressure. The firmer the pressure used to draw, the thicker the line appears.

Surfing

Exploring the Internet.

Surge protector

A controller to protect the computer and make up for variances in voltage.

Telnet

A way to communicate with a remote computer over a network.

Trackball

Input device that controls the position of the cursor on the screen; the unit is mounted near the keyboard, and movement is controlled by moving a ball.

Terabytes (TB)

A thousand gigabytes.

Teraflop

A measure of a computer's speed. It can be expressed as a trillion floating-point operations per second.

Trojan Horse

See **virus**.

UNIX

A very powerful operating system used as the basis of many high-end computer applications.

Upload

The process of transferring information from a computer to a web site (or other remote location on a network). To transfer information from a computer to a web site (or other remote location on a network).

URL

Uniform Resource Locator.

The protocol for identifying a document on the Web.

A Web address (e.g., www.tutorialspoint.com). A URL is unique to each user. See also domain.

UPS

Universal Power Supply or Uninterruptible Power Supply. An electrical power supply that includes a battery to provide enough power to a computer during an outage to back-up data and properly shut down.

USB

A multiple-socket USB connector that allows several USB-compatible devices to be connected to a computer.

USENET

A large unmoderated and unedited bulletin board on the Internet that offers thousands of forums, called newsgroups. These range from newsgroups exchanging information on scientific advances to celebrity fan clubs.

User friendly

A program or device whose use is intuitive to people with a non-technical background.

Video teleconferencing

A remote "face-to-face chat," when two or more people using a webcam and an Internet telephone connection chat online. The webcam enables both live voice and video.

Virtual reality (VR)

A technology that allows one to experience and interact with images in a simulated three-dimensional environment. For example, you could design a room in a house on your computer and actually feel that you are walking around in it even though it was never built. (The Holodeck in the science-fiction TV series Star Trek : Voyager would be the ultimate virtual reality.) Current technology requires the user to wear a special helmet, viewing goggles, gloves, and other equipment that transmits and receives information from the computer.

Virus

An unauthorized piece of computer code attached to a computer program or portions of a computer system that secretly copies itself from one computer to another by shared discs and over telephone and cable lines. It can destroy information stored on the computer, and in extreme cases, can destroy operability. Computers can be protected from viruses if the operator utilizes good virus prevention software and keeps the virus definitions up to date. Most viruses are not programmed to spread themselves. They have to be sent to another computer by e-mail, sharing, or applications. The worm is an exception, because it is programmed to replicate itself by sending copies to other computers listed in the e-mail address book in the computer. There are many kinds of viruses, for example:

> Boot viruses place some of their code in the start-up disk sector to automatically execute when booting. Therefore, when an infected machine boots, the virus loads and runs.

> File viruses attached to program files (files with the extension .exe). When you run the infected program, the virus code executes.

> Macro viruses copy their macros to templates and/or other application document files.

> Trojan Horse is a malicious, security-breaking program that is disguised as something being such as a screen saver or game.

> Worm launches an application that destroys information on your hard drive. It also sends a copy of the virus to everyone in the computer's e-mail address book.

WAV

A sound format (pronounced wave) used to reproduce sounds on a computer.

Webcam

A video camera/computer setup that takes live images and sends them to a Web browser.

Window

A portion of a computer display used in a graphical interface that enables users to select commands by pointing to illustrations or symbols with a mouse. "Windows" is also the name Microsoft adopted for its popular operating system.

World Wide Web ("WWW" or "the Web")

A network of servers on the Internet that use hypertext-linked databases and files. It was developed in 1989 by Tim Berners-Lee, a British computer scientist, and is now the primary platform of the Internet. The feature that distinguishes the Web from other Internet applications is its ability to display graphics in addition to text.

Word processor

A computer system or program for setting, editing, revising, correcting, storing, and printing text.

WYSIWYG

What You See Is What You Get. When using most word processors, page layout programs (See desktop publishing), and web page design programs, words and images will be displayed on the monitor as they will look on the printed page or web page.

End of Updated Computer Extended Glossary.

THE ALU GRAPHICS. ___

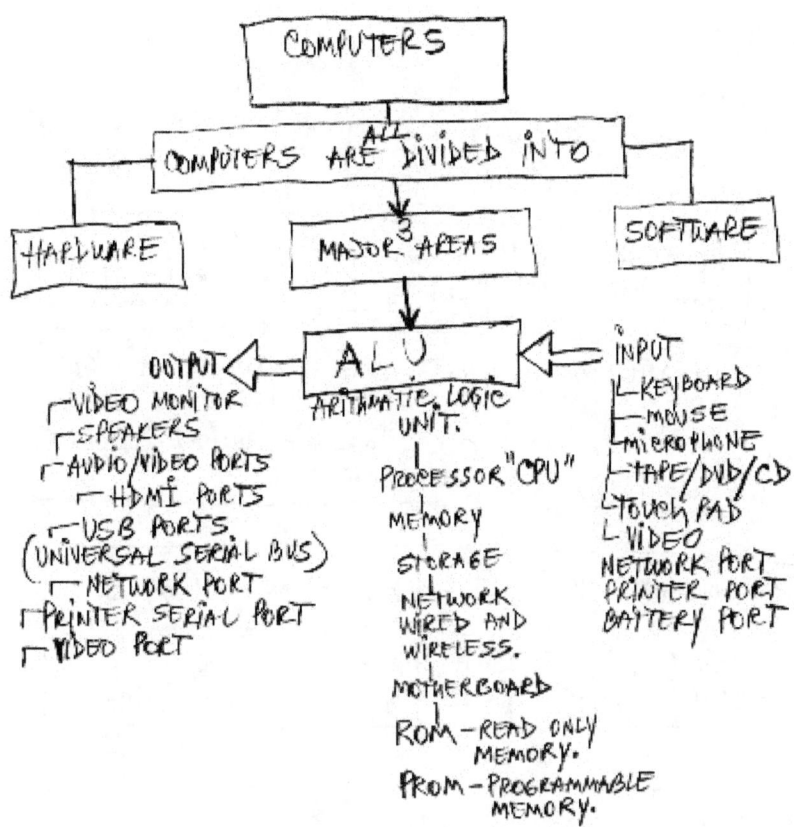

GRAPHICS PAGE 2.

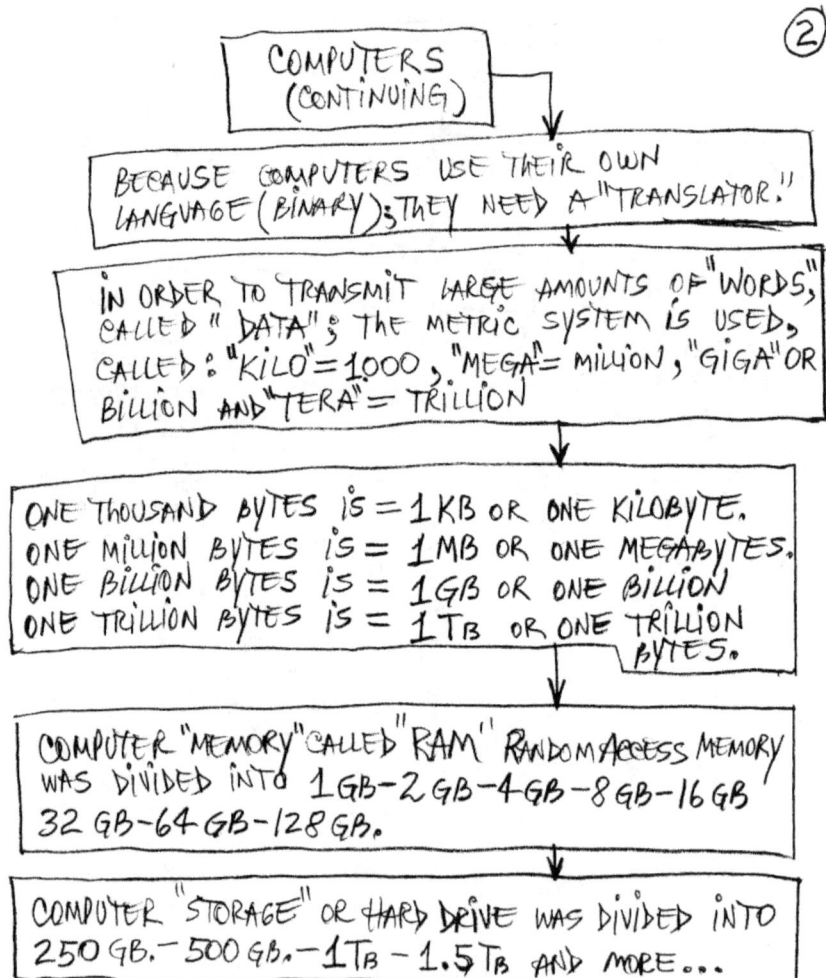

WINDOWS 10 GRAPHIC DIVISION.

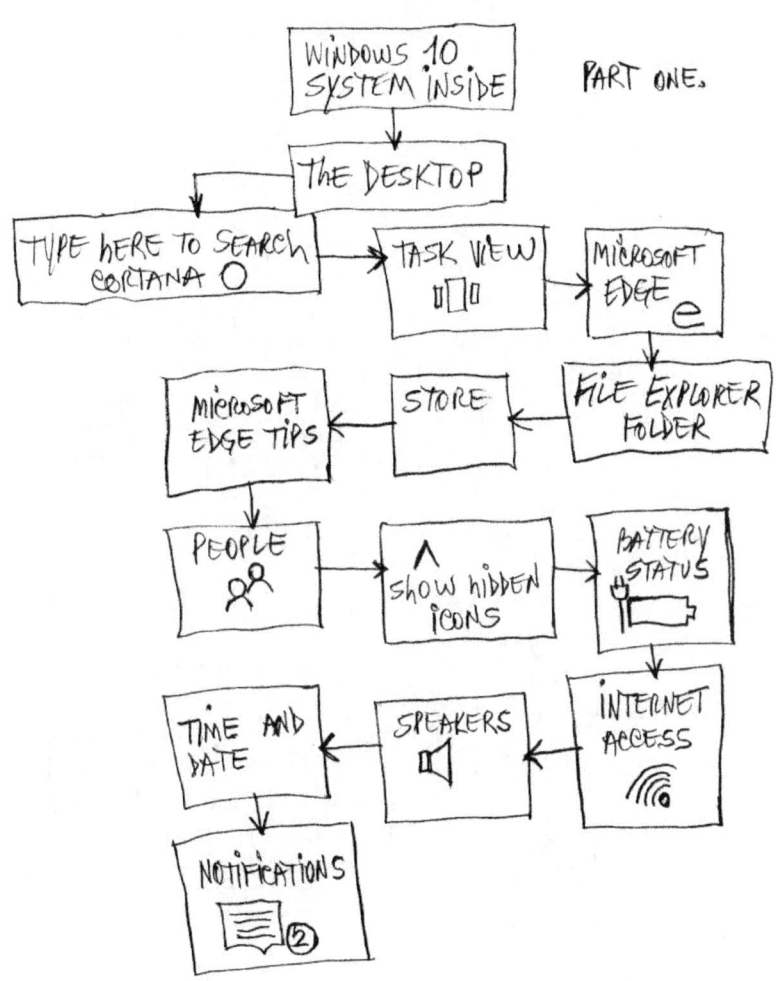

Dr ALFONSO J. KINGLOW

PART TWO.

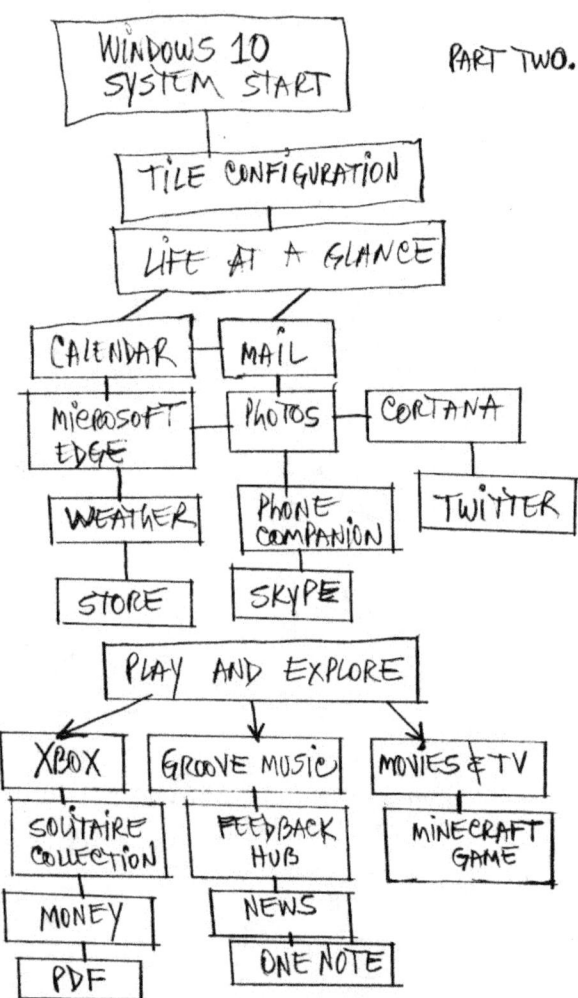

PART THREE

COMPUTER SURVIVAL KIT FOR SENIORS AND BEGINNERS REV 2

2018 COPYRIGHT © ALFONSO J. KINGLOW

Dr ALFONSO J. KINGLOW

NOTES.

7 BASIC USER TOOLS

Basic User Tools included in this book.

1. More Performance from Windows 10
2. How to Shutdown Windows correctly
3. The basic DIAX Diagnostic Tool
4. Create the hidden Advance Folder for Users
5. Protecting Computers from Viruses
6. What is a Virus
7. The Anti-Virus Programs to Protect Computers
8. Windows 10 Keyboard Shortcuts

MORE PERFORMANCE FROM WINDOWS. ___

To Get more Performance from Windows. Type: **sysdm.cpl** in the Start window search, lower left

using the **RUN** command; Goto Advanced tab, Goto Settings in the Performance tab, Select: Adjust for better Performance or Select: Adjust for best Appearance.

Or Select: Custom, and select your own preferences. When finish, click on Apply. And **Exit.**

How to Shutdown Windows 10 Computer Correctly. _

Slide to Shutdown.exe   Utility is Located in:

C:/ windows/system32 on the Hard Drive.

Goto the C:/drive

 Find the Windows folder

Inside of the *Windows* folder, search for the *System 32 folder.*

Inside of the System 32 folder search for the file: *"slide to shutdown,"*

drag it to your Desktop, or copy it to the desktop.

Copy the utility to the Desktop.

Double click to Shutdown the Computer by *Sliding downward* the arrow on the curtain like image. *Your Computer will Shutdown Immediately.*

Hidden Code(s) in Windows. ____

One of many..

Windows built in **Hidden Code** for Fixing and Troubleshooting <u>all parts of your PC.</u> By creating a Special <u>**Advanced Folder**</u> . like the Control Panel Icon.

Create the **Advanced. Folder:**

Then type the Code exactly, with **Open** and **Closed** Brackets like this { } and not [ ] .

Start:

Create a New Folder

Give it a name: **Advanced.**

Put a period after the d.

Enter the **Code** exactly:

Advanced. {ED7BA470-8E54-465E-825C-99712043E01C} <ENTER>

<u>The new green folder will be created</u> containing **237** files with graphics showing the User where, when, and why to Fix all and any problems with Windows.

What is a Virus
What are Viruses.

A Virus is any Program that do harm to your Computer. One of the method it uses is called Denial of Service or (DOS).
The different types of Viruses are: **ROOTKIT, TROJAN, WORM, MAIWARE, ADAWARE, SPAMM. HOAX, ETC..**

The first group will damage your computer, the second group will Reduce the Performance of the Computer, the third group or Hoax will Damage your Computer and take over your Email.

To Protect the Computer you will need an **ANTIVIRUS** Program or Application, <u>installed physically on the Computer Hardware its protecting.</u>
They are many different ANTIVIRUS programs, that are FREE and PAID. The **FREE** Antivirus **AVG** is Recommended. For larger Systems, the User can Buy the Paid version if they wish, but; The FREE Version works very well for most Users.

The Antivirus program will Block the DOS from the Virus and also initiate (SD) Routines, Seek and Destroy, All ERR or All Level Erradicate, and D/P Routines; Delete and Purge Immediately.

Microsoft created a special Tool that is called: **MRT** <u>Malicious Removal Tool.</u> That is **FREE** and can be downloaded from Microsoft.com install it on the Computer

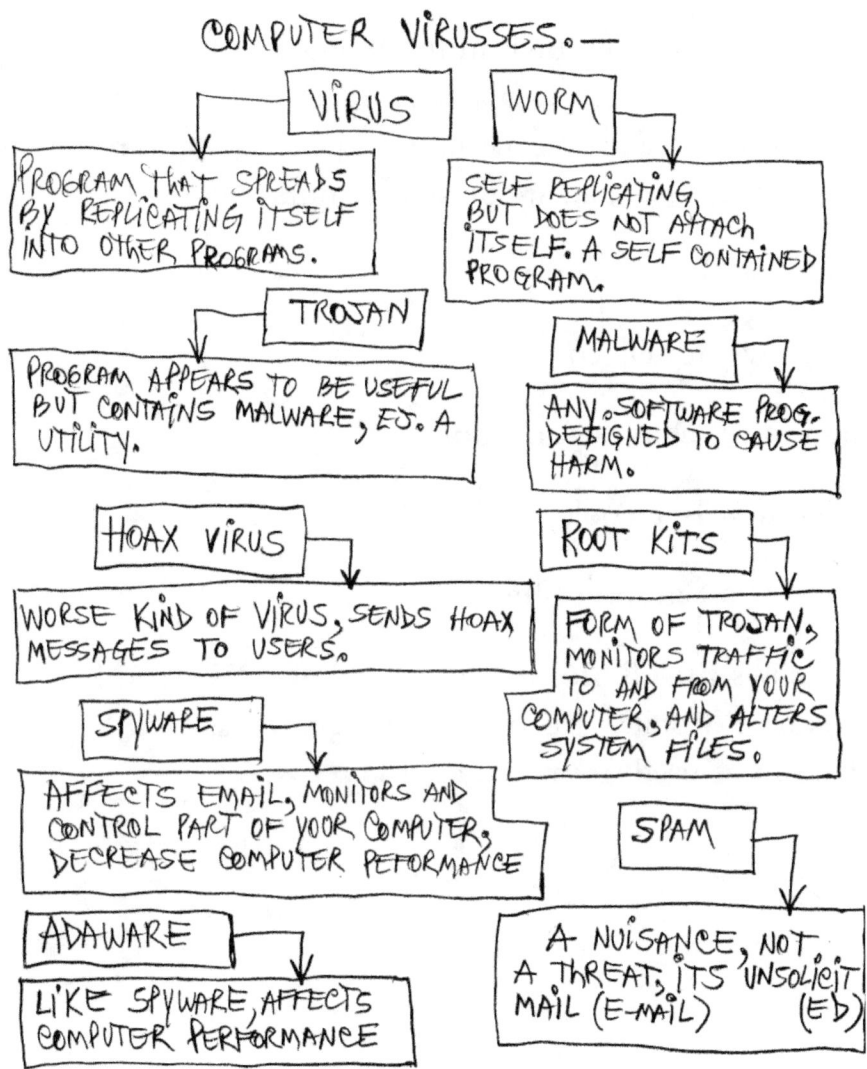

Windows Extended Tools

Windows Tools are built in the Windows Operating System and are available to the Users to troubleshoot and fix computer problems. Some <u>tools are hidden,</u> and are presented in this book.

Windows System Tools

Windows Admin Tools

Windows Diagnostic Tools

Windows User Tools

Windows Explorer Shell

Windows **PERF Monitor** and Windows **RESMON** Resource Monitor are available to the users as APP that can be used from the Desktop.

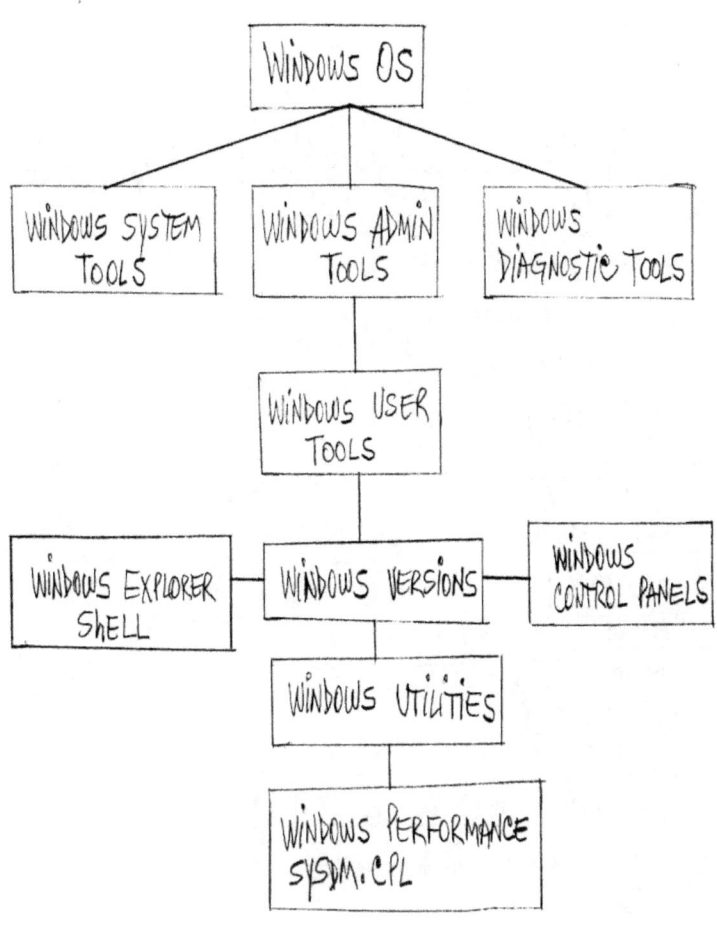

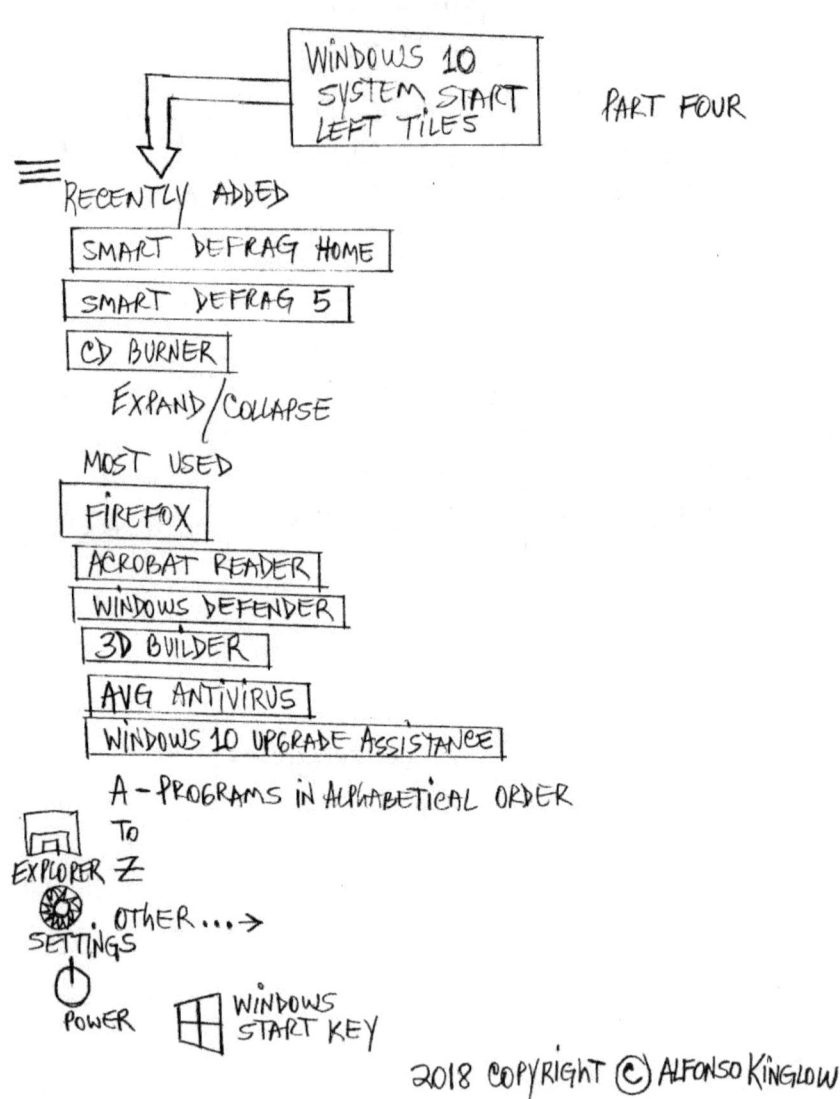

Semantic Search and the Semantic Web.__

While *Semantic Web* and *Semantic Search* are not the same thing, the two concepts are often confused.

The fact that these two families of technologies share the word *semantic* has led to some confusion about the difference between them. According to MerriamWebster, semantic means "of or related to meaning." Both of these kinds of technologies attempt to retrieve and present information based on its meaning rather than on its structure or intended usage, as more traditional technologies do. Although they are related, the two technologies in fact solve different problems.

In brief, Semantic Search is useful for searching on a single type of data in a single domain, whereas Semantic Web technologies are useful for querying <u>across many types of related information</u>. Consider a few examples of each kind of technology.

Although Google generally does a good job in ranking web pages, most of us know that this kind of search completely fails in other contexts. For example, searching your own computer for a document by relying on keywords can be very frustrating—not to mention searching a data store the size of your corporate intranet! In such cases, you will not succeed unless you know exactly what you are looking for. This shortfall is not the fault of the technology itself;

This is where Semantic Search comes in. Rather than blindly returning anything that contains the text you typed into the search bar, Semantic Search takes into account the *context* of your search as well as the underlying meaning of the documents to be searched.

However, what if you were searching for *jaguar*, the predatory black feline? Or *Jaguar*, the Mac 10.2 operating system? Or *Jaguar*, the Atari system? Even on Google, straightforward keyword searching <u>does not take into account the context of your</u>

search, nor does it understand the meaning of the documents.

In an attempt to do a better job, Semantic Search technologies employ various methods (NLP, statistical modeling, etc.), to categorize and/or cluster related documents to ease searching.

Semantic Web.

The Semantic Web is a set of technologies for representing, storing, and querying information. Although these technologies *can* be used to store textual data—such as text in a Word document or PDF file—they typically are used to store smaller bits of data. Thus, while Semantic Search focuses largely on textual information, **the Semantic Web** also includes numbers, dates, figures, and other data in addition to text.

Semantic Web and Semantic Search Combined

Generally speaking, anything that can be accomplished with Semantic Search can be represented as a Semantic Web query. That is, Semantic Web technologies are sufficiently broad to encompass all Semantic Search capabilities.

A simple way to think about which family of technologies might be useful for a specific problem is to ask yourself whether your users are searching on only one kind of information (e.g., restaurants, a flight number, etc.), or whether they are searching on many kinds of information (e.g., which presidents had children who did not live in the White House).

Semantic Web vendors focus on solving problems using many different kinds of information. Instead of simply storing data about restaurants, <u>a Semantic Web application would have access to information about the chefs, the cities, the menus, the cuisine styles, the décor, the wine list, the wineries that produced the wine on the wine list, etc.</u>

However, if you need to answer a question such as, "What restaurants in Boston have several wines that were produced in the Alsace region between 1998 and 2001?" then

Semantic Search will not be able to help you; instead, <u>you will need the Semantic Web</u>.

More about setting up the Computer's Hardware and CMD command. __

The Hardware is the box or frame that contains all the major parts of a computer, the internal hard drive, the CD/DVD Player, the different input ports, the keyboard and mouse, the processor and ram memory, the Ethernet network card, the Wireless network card, the video display, the LCD display(on laptops), the sound card, the internal built in camera, the internal microphone, etc.. One of the major Ports is the USB (Universal Serial Bus) that is now used to connect Printers, Cameras and multiple other devices to your computer hardware.

Policies every User should know, that are Built-in. __

Policies are built into the computer hardware to allow for security and to manage the hardware. Some of the most important policies are the **SECPOL. MSC (Security Policy) and GPEDIT. MSC (Group Policy Editor)** these policies allow you to setup the security configuration on your computer hardware. These policies are launched using the **Command Line (CMD)** built into your computer, or by typing the policy directly into the START or RUN line. The Command Line CMD is provided as a means of accessing your Computer Hardware and Software policies and to directly manage a great part of your computer hardware, without requiring any software to manage policies.

It is used also for direct maintenance of the computer and comes with a reasonable help file. This file contains all of the commands used with the **CMD.** The command line window when launched appears with a black background. The background and text colors can be changed from a menu of different colors as well as the text size and window size. Some preferred combinations are; red background with yellow text color or green background with white or purple text color, etc… To change the color background and text, click on the CMD icon in the upper left side of the command window.

Access and MMC. __

To access all of the standard policies to set up your computer hardware you can find them in the **MMC (Microsoft Management Console) built into your Computer hardware.**

> The **MMC** allow the user to create Snap-in's to setup the hardware and security configuration. To access the MMC just type it into the CMD window or directly into the START or RUN line, on the lower left side of your computer.
>
> > A View of Computer Configuration with Applications and Utilities. ____
> >
> > The User Tools and System Tools are presented in a
> > Graphic configuration easy to understand. All the Diagnostic Tools that are built-into Windows are shown and are available to the user, for diagnostics and troubleshooting the computer.

USER DIAGNOSTIC TOOLS.

(12) Twelve Diagnostic Tools are shown that are built into Windows. All these tools can be access by the user.

If the Computer is running Windows 10, just type in the name of the tool in Cortana, to access, or just type the name into the Start area for all other Systems.

8 MORE PERFORMANCE FROM WINDOWS

To get <u>more Performance and Appearance from Windows</u>
To Get more Performance from Windows. Type:

sysdm.cpl

using the **RUN** <u>command</u>; Goto <u>Advanced tab,</u> Goto <u>Settings</u> in the Performance tab, Select: <u>Adjust for better Performance</u> or Select: **Adjust for best Appearance.**

Or Select: <u>Custom,</u> and select your own Preferences. When finish, click on <u>Apply</u>. And Exit.

Windows Shortcuts and Utilities. __

SHIFT + F8 when Computer is Booting, To Access " SAFE MODE" to fix Computer

Windows Key + X for Special MENU

Open RUN and Type in: Shell:AppsFolder To Access the " All Applications" Folder

<u>Utility</u> to Shutdown Windows Correctly. __

"Slide to Shutdown" Windows Utility, is located in: C:>/windows/system32/slide to shutdown.exe on the Hard Drive.

Copy the utility to the desktop and Shutdown Windows correctly by pulling down the curtain like from the pointed arrow.

TO KEEP YOUR COMPUTER CLEAN AND ENHANCE PERFORMANCE AND ELIMINATE MALWARE, ADAWARE AND SPYWARE. ___

FREE SPECIAL USER UTILITIES.

Download the following Utilities and RUN them at least Once a Week or every Two weeks.

Advanced System Care 14

Glary Utility 5.135

Clean Master 6.0

Acebyte Utility 3.2

AVG free Antivirus

Dr ALFONSO J. KINGLOW

BASIC INFORMATION ABOUT WINDOWS USER TOOLS.

Windows User Tools, continuing..

Command prompt (CMD)

Control Panel

Resource Monitor (RESMON)

Performance Monitor (PERFMON)

Run Command

Slide to Shutdown

System Information

System Configuration

Task Manager **CTRL+ALT+DEL**

Safe Mode Shift + F8

Special Menu Windows Key + "X" Key

Shell

Explorer Shell

Extended Windows Diagnostic Tools:

MSConfig from RUN

3D Builder

      Narrator

      Performance monitor

      Resource Monitor

      RUN Command

      System Configuration

      Task Manager

Windows Extended System Tools:

1. On Screen Keyboard
2. Phone companion
3. Phone
4. System Information

5. Uninstall

6. Windows memory Diagnostic

7. Win Patrol Explorer

8. Win Patrol Help

9. CMD Command Line

Windows Administrative (ADMIN) Tools

Computer Management

Defragment drives

Disk Cleanup

Event Viewer

ISCSI Initiator

Local Security Policy

ODBC Data Sources

Performance Monitor

Print Management

Recovery Drive

Resource Monitor

Windows Services Tools. __

System Configuration

System Information

Task Scheduler

Windows Defender Firewall

Windows Memory Diagnostic (**DXDIAG**)

Explorer Shell.

USING EXPLORER SHELL. TO CREATE A PORTABLE FOLDER OF ANY PART OF WINDOWS SYSTEMS. ____

USING " EXPLORER SHELL"

Create a Short Cut Folder by selecting NEW and Shortcut

In the Shortcut window: Type: Explorer Shell: and the name of the Part of Windows you want to create: for Example:

>   Explorer Shell:ControlPanelFolder

and click NEXT   another window will be displayed.

Type the name you want to give to the folder, and press <Finish>

The new Control Panel Folder will be created.

Another Example: Explorer Shell:AppsFolder   The All Applications Folder will be Created.

1. This folder will be portable and can be used on any Windows Computer.

SOME WINDOWS SHELL COMMANDS.__

You can use any of the following commands to create the desired shortcut:

explorer shell:MyComputerFolder (for My Computer   shortcut) explorer shell:RecycleBinFolder (for Recycle Bin shortcut) explorer shell:ControlPanelFolder (for Control Panel shortcut) explorer shell:Administrati Tools (for Administrative Tools shortcut) explorer shell:ChangeRemoveProgramsFolder (for Programs and Features shortcut) explorer shell:NetworkPlacesFolder (for Network shortcut) explorer shell:Favorites (for Favorites shortcut) explorer shell:HomegroupFolder (for Homegroup shortcut) explorer shell:Games (for Games shortcut) explorer shell:Fonts (for Fonts shortcut) explorer shell:UserProfiles (for Users folder shortcut) explorer shell:Profile (for your username folder shortcut) explorer shell:Public (for Public folder shortcut) explorer shell:My Documents (for Documents shortcut) explorer shell:Common Documents (for Public Documents shortcut)

explorer shell:My Music (for Music folder shortcut) explorer shell:CommonMusic (for Public Music folder shortcut) explorer shell:My Pictures (for Pictures folder shortcut) explorer shell:CommonPictures (for Public
    Pictures folder shortcut) explorer shell:My Video (for Videos folder shortcut) explorer shell:CommonVideo (forPublicVideos

9 SHUTDOWN WINDOWS TOOL

How to Shutdown Windows 10 Computer Correctly. _

Slide to Shutdown.exe   Utility is Located in:

C:/ windows/system32 on the Hard Drive.

Goto the C:/drive

Find the Windows folder

Inside of the *Windows* folder, search for the *System 32 folder.*

Inside of the System 32 folder search for the file: *"slide to shutdown,"*

drag it to your Desktop, or copy it to the desktop.

Copy the utility to the Desktop.

Double click to Shutdown the Computer by *Sliding downward* the arrow on the curtain like image. *Your Computer will Shutdown Immediately.*

SLIDE TO SHUTDOWN APPLICATION. __

Get the Application at C:/windows/system 32 on the hard drive, look inside the system 32 folder for the file: **SlideToShutDown.exe**

Copy the file application to the desktop., you can also create a blank folder, and copy the application with the copy command, and Paste it into the blank folder and name the folder: WINDOWS SHUTDOWN..

To Shutdown Windows, just doubleclick the Application " SlideToShutdown.exe "
and drag the bottom arrow downward like closing a blind or curtain. Windows will then Shutdown Immediately. No waiting to Shutdown.

10 HIDDEN CODES IN WINDOWS

Extended Hidden Code(s) in Windows. _____

One of the hidden Codes in Windows.

Windows built in **Hidden Codes** for Fixing and Troubleshooting <u>all parts of your PC.</u> By creating a Special **Advanced Folder** like a Control Panel.

Create the **Advanced. Folder:**

Then type the Code exactly, with **Open** and **Closed** Brackets like this { } and not [ ] .

Start:

Create a New Folder

Give it a name: **Advanced.**

Put a period after the d.

Enter the **Code** exactly:

Advanced. {ED7BA470-8E54-465E-825C-99712043E01C} <ENTER>

The new green folder will be created containing **237** files with graphics showing the user where, when, and why to Fix all and any problems with Windows.

This folder is normally hidden and can only be created with the proper Code.
The Code is typed after the empty folder is created.

They are many hidden Codes in windows that empower the Users to fix and troubleshoot their computer systems if they know where to go.

This book presents the information that users need and the knowledge about their Computer Hardware and Software to fix any problems with the hardware and the system software.

It hopes to provide all of the knowledge Users and beginners as well as Seniors and Empowers everyone to know everything about their own Computer hardware and Software.
This Book assumes that the Reader and User knows very little about Computer Systems and provides the necessary knowledge that they can implement themselves.

NOTES.

ABOUT THE AUTHOR

This is the first Book of Survival Kit, that shares Professor Kinglow vision in bringing modern Technology to all Users as well as Seniors and Beginners trying to keep up with Computer Technology, in a very basic and comprehensive format that is easy to understand. The basic and hidden Tools presented in this book will allow the user to setup the Computer correctly and use all the built in tools to provide the max performance and to empower the users and beginners to better understand how the Computer works and how to use the tools that are provided to keep the computer secure and implement hidden Security configurations, now available to users and beginners.

The book is written in a format intended to provide information that will help Users Survive most problems they could have with their Computers during this Pandemic, that they could check and fix themselves, during this time period where it would be difficult to go out and or find someone to work on the machine.

It contains Graphic figures in a box format that makes it easy to convey the information, not just in text mode. The book contains all the built-in System Tools, and hidden System and User Tools to Empower the Users and beginners to better understand their Computer Hardware and Software, and to be able to Maintain and troubleshoot their own Computer Systems and Applications.

With information on the new WI-Fi Standards and other updated Systems and information for 2021 and 2022.

Dr Kinglow is the Author of many Books, which are available on **Amazon.com, Lulu.com**, and Barnes Noble Book Stores.

Professor Kinglow received his PhD and many other Awards and Commendations, and is the author of many Technical innovations published. He received the October 2013 Volunteer Spotlight Award from The City of Las Cruces, NM. and is featured in "Las Cruces Magazine" published by real View publishing, Las Cruces New Mexico.

He started Computer Classes for Seniors and Beginners, at **Munson Senior Center**, in Las Cruces, NM., and at **Shadow Mountain Senior Center** in Phoenix, Arizona where he and his wife are Active Volunteers.

Dr. Kinglow have taught overseas at various

Universities as a bilingual visiting Professor, and is a Systems Engineer by trade. While working for **NASA** he received the NASA STS-34 Award for outstanding dedication and Mission Support for the Galileo Mission and others. Dr. Kinglow received many Commendations and Honors from NASA for his support of the Shuttle Missions., and many Scientific Contributions. He is a Member of IEEE and The Computer Society.

" A closed Book have no Power."

Dr. Alfonso J. Kinglow PhD

Those that Travel, read a Book, Those that don't Travel read a Page. "

www.ingramcontent.com/pod-product-compliance
Lightning Source LLC
Chambersburg PA
CBHW060845170526
45158CB00001B/241